The Other Side of the
Asian American Success Story

Wendy Walker-Moffat

The Other Side of the Asian American Success Story

Jossey-Bass Publishers
San Francisco

Substantial discounts on bulk quantities of Jossey-Bass books are available to corporations, professional associations, and other organizations. For details and discount information, contact the special sales department at Jossey-Bass Inc., Publishers. (415) 433–1740; Fax (800) 605–2665.

For sales outside the United States, please contact your local Paramount Publishing International Office.

 Manufactured in the United States of America on Lyons Falls Pathfinder Tradebook. This paper is acid-free and 100 percent totally chlorine-free.

Library of Congress Cataloging-in-Publication Data

Walker-Moffat, Wendy, date–
    The other side of the Asian American success story / Wendy Walker
-Moffat — 1st ed.
        p.   cm. — (The Jossey-Bass education series)
    Includes bibliographical references (p.   ) and index.
    ISBN 0-7879-0122-9
    1. Hmong Americans—Education.   2. Home and school—United States.
3. Multicultural education—United States.   4. Hmong (Asian people)—
Social life and customs.   I. Title.   II. Series.
LC3501.H56W35   1995
371.9795--dc20   95-21568
                                                                                                    CIP

FIRST EDITION
HB Printing   10 9 8 7 6 5 4 3 2 1

To Walter H. Walker III:
the best role model a sister could have

Contents

Contents

Preface

As Americans, we are all survivors, whether our families were dislocated by the arrival of Europeans, were forced to come involuntarily from Africa, or came by choice or necessity from elsewhere. Survival marks us all. This book looks at the Hmong, a seemingly exotic people from the mountains of Laos, who are refugees from the Vietnam War that also enveloped their country. By learning about these survivors, readers of this book can begin to examine what is now being taught in our schools to newcomers, and to consider why a sound educational theory that connects home and school knowledge is needed. The period of post–World War II prosperity has ended. Americans now face the challenge of the twenty-first century: to recognize that our diversity is a strength rather than a weakness. Schools are one of the few places where we can influence the behavior, attitudes, and knowledge of future generations. Family-based multicultural education is a theory that promises to help us make the most of our strength.

Many of the findings conveyed in this book emerged from my examination of two school districts at opposite ends of the country, one in New England and one in California. These findings point to the need for schools to work with the families of students on a daily basis, to integrate family knowledge into the curriculum, to draw on family strengths, and to use these strengths to reshape schools to respond to the survival needs of students. I believe that the home–school connection is the key to the challenge of recognizing that our diversity is a strength.

These conclusions are not limited to the Hmong; they apply to students from most Southeast Asian refugee families, as well to the children of other immigrant families. They have implications for the development of national educational policies for family literacy, for administrator and teacher development, for the preparation of guidance counselors, and for the careers of bicultural classroom aides and paraprofessional counselors. They have implications for state and school district policies on multicultural programs and classes in English as a Second Language (ESL). They have implications for daily activities and interactions in all classrooms.

They also have international implications. Education has always been a strong arm of U.S. foreign policy, particularly in Southeast Asia, where one of the unheralded successes of American efforts in Vietnam and Laos in the 1960s was the establishment of primary and secondary schools in rural areas where there had previously been few or no schools. As unprecedented migration and changing fertility rates alter the demographics of the world, the United States stands poised to become a leader in multicultural education. This potential is based on the history of education in this country, a history that entails the successes and failures of educational programs developed to meet the challenges of immigration and cultural diversity.

Much of this book is an outgrowth of my 1989 doctoral thesis for Harvard University, "Challenges of the Hmong Culture: A Study of Teacher, Counselor, and Administrator Training in a Time of Changing Demographics." The Hmong in the United States have been the focus of my research because they are an extreme example of the challenges faced by public schools. Since the Hmong have concentrated in a few places in the country, their impact on the schools in these areas is larger than their national impact. Although anthropologists often study people of other cultures, I did not choose to study the Hmong in order to become an anthropologist. Rather, I needed to learn about the qualitative research methods used by anthropologists, such as Clifford Geertz and other social scientists, in order to better understand the "webs of significance" (Geertz, 1973, p. 5) of the Hmong culture and political history.

I began my work with the Hmong in 1981 in Seattle, Washington, on a project designed to help Hmong refugees become farmers again. In January 1983, I decided to broaden my focus by moving to Thailand. My first job, at the Phanat Nikom refugee camp, was to teach job-related language skills to Hmong and other preliterate refugees who were bound for the United States. The Hmong were the reason I then moved to northeast Thailand to work at the Ban Vinai refugee camp near the Mekong River on the Laotian border. Despite the remoteness of the camp—getting there entailed an overnight bus ride from Bangkok followed by a long trip along the Mekong River road to the camp—and the fact that I was a single European American woman, I felt safe working with the Hmong. Among certain families, I was trusted and loved as a sister.

Ban Vinai was the largest refugee camp in Thailand at the time, housing approximately forty-five thousand refugees from the mountains of Laos, most of them Hmong. Many of the Hmong there refused to go to the United States. They had heard that life was difficult there and they wanted to return to Laos. Working to secure financial support for a refugee farm project, I began to understand the importance for the Hmong of traditional farming procedures, self-sufficiency, and survival. While conducting a nutrition study of children less than five years old for the United Nations High Commissioner for Refugees, I worked closely with young Hmong women of childbearing years who were not yet married. We were faced by the same challenges to our abilities because of our gender and because we were single.

When I returned to the United States to study at the Harvard Graduate School of Education, I wanted to learn how Hmong students were doing in U.S. public schools. People I had known well in the refugee camps had come to the United States, providing me with a rare opportunity to observe a cultural transition over a ten-year period. Through work for the Ford Foundation and by participating in the national study of immigrant students conducted by the National Coalition of Advocates for Students (1988), I was able to visit school sites in New England, Washington, Texas, and California. Everyone I talked to said, "They're doing so well, we really do not need to worry about them." It soon became evident that it was not just the Hmong that schools were unconcerned about; it was Asians as a group.

Surprisingly little has been published about Southeast Asian refugee students and how they fit into the context of all Asian Americans and of all minority students. Research by Caplan, Whitmore, Bui, and Trautman (1985b) and by Caplan, Whitmore, and Choy (1989) caused quite a reaction in the education field because it found that even boat refugees were successful students. The problems with this research are pointed out in Chapter Three. What is different about my book is that, based on the experiences of the Hmong, it questions the accuracy of the Asian American success story.

The case of the Hmong challenges several prevalent theories that suggest that the academic motivation of minority students reflects their socioeconomic background. It also challenges the relevance of motivation theories. It points out how the commonly refuted deficit theory is the basis of some Sheltered English and ESL programs. This is the first book to highlight the lack of preparation of teachers, administrators, and guidance counselors for the challenges of multilingual and multicultural students. It also begins to fill the tremendous gap in the literature on how the Hmong community and other Southeast Asian refugees are involved in the schools as parents, teachers, counselors, and aides.

A primary purpose of the book is to show the danger of racism and inaccuracy in the Asian American success story by telling about the other side of Asian American academic success. It is a story about differences—in gender, in cultural priorities, in home support, and in achievement. This book offers a new perspective, a survival theory to explain the behavior of Hmong and other refugee students from Southeast Asia, as well as from other non-European countries. It outlines the promise of family-based multi-cultural education. It provides a model for paraprofessional bicultural counselors to meet the needs of students, of their parents, and of school administrators.

The book also calls attention to the problem of how federal immigration policy affects schools, particularly the effort to implement federal laws concerning the equal educational opportunities of those who are learning the English language. These laws have resulted in, among other problems, the states' obligation to provide educational programs they cannot afford to develop or implement properly. The real issue is a national question: can we face up to who we are and make appropriate changes in the classroom?

This book is addressed to policy makers, parents, teachers, administrators, guidance counselors, student/child advocates, and anyone in the general public who is interested in immigration, in the current diversity in U.S. public schools, and in what that diversity means in terms of student behavior, the quality of education, teacher preparation, and such social issues as teen pregnancy and the welfare dependency of young, new Americans. Academically, the book is addressed to scholars in the fields of education, policy studies, Asian American studies, ethnic studies, American studies, sociology, anthropology, social welfare, and refugee and immigration studies. It is also my hope that it will serve an overseas market, particularly Hong Kong, Taiwan, Korea, Malaysia, Singapore, and Thailand, where there is great interest in how American public schools respond to students from Asian backgrounds, as well as England and Europe, where classroom demographics are changing as rapidly as in the United States.

Overview of the Contents

The book begins with the story of a Hmong girl that illustrates the difficulties often encountered by Hmong and other Southeast Asian children in their efforts to pursue an American education. Si Chi's story sets the stage for the issues to be explored in the chapters that follow.

Chapter One provides a critical analysis of the amazing Asian American academic success story, including its basis in academic studies. The chapter reveals the distortion and misrepresentation of popular stereotypes.

Chapter Two explains who Asian Americans are and how this group has been dramatically changed since the late 1960s by changes in patterns of immigration to the United States. It introduces the major subgroups while at the same time countering the notion that all of their cultures can be subsumed under one category.

In Chapter Three I tell the story of what really happened when Hmong students first arrived in two school districts on opposite sides of the county, showing how teachers and administration responded to refugee youngsters and what resources were at their disposal.

Chapter Four focuses on how culture influences student behavior, particularly that of girls, and how that influence runs counter to existing theories about the importance of motivation in academic success.

Chapter Five analyzes the challenges that exist in schools as a result of the new demographics, and offers practical solutions. It examines ESL programs and the idea of bilingual education, as well as the impacts of segregation and standardized testing on the quality of education received by immigrant and refugee students.

In Chapter Six I offer a theory of family-based multicultural education to counter the deficit theories that have been at the root of schools' inadequate responses to the needs of the new immigrants. I offer extensive guidelines for putting the theory into practice. I also offer a model of how paraprofessional counselors can help school districts respond to the diversity in the student body that is not yet reflected in the faculty.

Finally, in the epilogue, I summarize all my findings around the concept that what matters in the education of Southeast Asian newcomers is not the methods teachers adopt but their attitudes toward their students' cultural differences, which they should regard as strengths rather than as deficits.

Acknowledgments

During the years of this book's evolution I have been helped and supported by many people. I wish to recognize a few of them. First, I want to thank Vang Ger, Vang Thai, Joua, Waa, and all the Hmong who have helped and included me in their families' lives. I wish to acknowledge the love and support of my family. Neither of my sons, Corey or Keith, were alive when I began this research. Their arrival impressed upon me how difficult it is to be a mother and pursue an education, one of the key topics of this book. Through them I also became intimately aware of the high quality of child care developed by mountain cultures in Laos. I especially want to thank my husband, David Moffat, for his skillful and thoughtful editing. His valuable insights have helped convert a doctoral thesis into a book that is readable. I wish to acknowledge my mother, Irene Walker. Without her encouragement, I would not have gone to Harvard. I wish to thank my Hmong friends and family for their love and support in Thailand and in the United States. I also want to thank Father Edward Brady, S.J., and to remember David Belskis, Director of Save the Children in Thailand. These two men made tremendous contributions to the education of refugees in Southeast Asia. In so doing, they introduced me to issues of education for refugees in Thailand based on their experiences, and advanced my level of knowledge beyond my years.

I wish to acknowledge the financial support of the Ford Foundation, and the pragmatic guidance of the late chief program officer for this research, Edward J. Meade. I want to thank ARC Associates of Oakland, California. The executive director, Sau-Lim Tsang, and director of development, Virginia Lim, have tirelessly read endless drafts of various chapters, and perhaps most importantly, provided moral courage. Pierina Wong, site director for the Multifunctional Resource Center for Southern California, and Janet Lu, president of the National Association for Asian and Pacific American Education, also provided valuable insights. Ronald Podeschi's review of the manuscript was very helpful. I wish to thank my doctoral committee at Harvard: the late Paul Ylvisaker, who was the first person to say my work was publishable; Joseph Maxwell, who read every word I ever asked him to and was always able to provide a fresh perspective; and Merry White, who was always positive and supportive. Finally, I would like to thank my adviser Harold Howe, II, "Doc," for his wisdom and sense of humor. When I feared that my critique of ESL programs might be poorly received or, even worse, taken out of context to be used against the development of genuine bilingual programs that I support fully, it was Doc who said, "Hold your nose and jump in." Well, Doc, here goes!

All names and places are pseudonyms.

Berkeley, California   Wendy Walker-Moffat
June 1995

⊚⊘ The Author

Wendy Walker-Moffat is an Affiliated Scholar at Stanford University in the Institute for Research on Women and Gender. She also lectures at the University of California, Berkeley, in the School of Social Welfare, on policy issues related to immigrants and refugees. Walker-Moffat's primary research activities have focused on the education and fertility rates of refugee and immigrant women and their children. She worked in refugee camps and villages in Thailand for three years. She conducted a nutrition study for the United Nations High Commissioner for Refugees. She redesigned and secured the funding for a farm project for Hmong refugees at Ban Vinai refugee camp and nearby Thai villagers. She also taught U.S.-bound refugees and wrote grant proposals for a preschool and for a women's center for Cambodian, Lao, Hmong, and Mien refugees at the Phanat Nikom refugee camp.

In 1994, Walker received a Southeast Asian Ford Foundation Grant to teach a course on Southeast Asian refugee women during the Trinity Term and in the International Summer Institute at Oxford University in the Refugee Studies Programme. In the spring of 1994 she also received a Technical Assistance Grant from the California Policy Seminar to report on the fertility rates and use of public services by Mexican women who had recently immigrated to the United States. The University of California, Berkeley,

Chicano/Latino Policy Project awarded her a mini-grant for related research.

Walker-Moffat earned her B.A. (1979) in international relations from Brown University, her M.Phil. (1981) in international development from the Institute of Development Studies at Sussex University, United Kingdom, and her Ed.D. (1989) in administration, planning, and social policy at Harvard University's Graduate School of Education. She worked for ARC Associates of Oakland, California, from 1991 to 1993. She was part of a two-year national study of children of immigrant and refugee families for the National Coalition of Advocates for Students, funded by the Ford Foundation. She worked for the Laotian Educational Council in Richmond, California, and California Tomorrow. Internationally, she has worked for the United Nations High Commissioner for Refugees, the American Refugee Committee, Save the Children, World Education, the Consortium, CARE, Food for the Hungry, and the Catholic Organization for Emergency Relief and Refugees, a Thai organization. She is also a consultant to the Ford Foundation. Walker-Moffat is a member of the Women's Commission for Refugee Women and Children. She is married to David Moffat. They have two sons, Corey Maxwell and Keith Alexander, and live in Berkeley, California.

The Other Side of the Asian American Success Story

Prologue: A Story About Difference

This is a story about the other side of Asian American academic success. It is a story about difference: differences in gender, in cultural priorities, in home support, and in achievement. To begin, I would like to tell the tale of one Hmong girl, Si Chi, that illustrates the difficulties such children often encounter if they want to pursue their education. Si Chi's story also introduces some of the mixed messages inherent in our school system about girls and the cultural and gender blinders frequently worn by school administrators.

As is customary among the Hmong, Si Chi's marriage to Lee Foung was arranged by her father and Lee Foung's older brother. Si Chi had little say in the process; she was only thirteen years old. The basis of the marriage negotiations was that Lee Foung wanted to come to the United States and Si Chi's family had already been accepted for resettlement. After their marriage, in time Lee Foung and Si Chi developed a relationship of love. In the United States, at the age of fifteen, Si Chi was regarded as an adult by fellow Hmong. She was proud to be married. Many of her Hmong friends envied her. Si Chi said that before she was married, school and home responsibilities were of equal importance. After she married, but before she had a baby, education was her top priority. After having a baby, however, the baby became all-important. Instead of going to school, she was expected to keep her family's apartment clean, entertain her husband's friends, prepare traditional Hmong meals, do the laundry, care for their child, and continue having babies, preferably sons.

Had Si Chi grown up in Laos, she probably would not have attended school at all, or only for a few years at best. Instead, she was one of a few Hmong girls who completed all six grades in the primary school at Ban Vinai Refugee Camp in Thailand. Si Chi exemplifies the tension that education has introduced into the traditional role of Hmong women. Si Chi is caught between being a typical Hmong woman and being an American teenager. While she was pregnant, and after giving birth the first time, she was frustrated by her confinement to the home. She anxiously awaited her friends' return from school so she could talk to them on the phone and find out what happened that day. Si Chi was jealous of her husband's two cousins, both boys, who were in her grade in school and who continued studying. Si Chi thought she was smarter than either of them, but their English and academic skills continued to grow while her's stagnated. Initially, Si Chi was anxious to return to school as soon as her baby was born, but her husband told her he was too busy to bring her. She would not go alone. Since then she has wavered back and forth about school.

School systems have not handled Si Chi well. Her family was originally resettled in Minnesota, where at age fourteen she was placed in the eighth grade. She liked school, had many Hmong girl-friends, and did well in English as a Second Language classes. But two months into the school year, her family decided to move to southern California. In early November, the local California school district placed her in the ninth grade because her Immigration and Naturalization Services card said she was fifteen years old, even though she was really fourteen by American years. The administrator at her school told her she could not enroll until February. Si Chi never enrolled in that school district because she and her husband moved north to join his relatives in another California community in December.

Once in the new school district, Si Chi was told she should go to adult school instead of completing the eighth grade, as she had requested. When she insisted on enrolling in junior high school, the administrator placed her in the ninth grade. Although her high placement scores showed that she could go directly into mainstream classes, she was encouraged to remain in the Newcomer Program because she was pregnant. A director of a teen-parenting resource center explained that the schools do not like to have pregnant girls in junior high school because "they [the administrators] think it is catchy."

In April, after two months in the eighth grade and three months in the ninth grade, Si Chi stopped going to school because her husband was afraid she would hurt herself and the unborn child on the crowded school bus. No one told her she could go on home study or independent study. Her baby was born in August. For five months she did little but watch television and help the wife of her husband's cousin with her little children. After the birth, the director of the Newcomer Program again suggested that Si Chi go to the adult school. No one told Si Chi or her husband that five of the high schools in the city had teen-parent programs with nursery facilities.

Si Chi's husband talked to the woman in charge of the teen-parenting program at the local high school in September. The woman said that he should take Si Chi to register in October. In October her husband brought Si Chi to meet the principal at the high school. The principal said Si Chi could start in the winter term. Again, no one provided Si Chi with a home-study program in the meantime. Si Chi wanted to enroll in November. The secretary at the high school said she could not enroll until the next quarter. When asked why Si Chi could not enroll immediately, the ninth grade guidance counselor assigned to students whose last name began with the same letter as Si Chi's said, "I don't have a girl of that name at this school." She then went on to explain that "it's very difficult. We don't have enough room" for new mothers. There were between fifty and sixty girls in the teen-mother program already. They were placed on a first-come, first-served basis.

Eventually, Si Chi's husband went to see another guidance counselor. He brought a letter from the director of the Newcomer Program. Si Chi was allowed to enroll in December in the ninth grade. She left her newborn daughter with her sister-in-law. Si Chi lasted two weeks. When her daughter came down with chicken pox, Si Chi stopped going to school. Again, no one contacted her or told her that she was eligible for home study. In her new apartment, Si Chi was isolated. There was no television or radio, only a tape deck. During the day, Si Chi read her husband's school books and took care of the baby. After two months of sitting at home while her husband attended school, she wanted to try going to school again, but her husband decided they would move to a small town further north where it was less expensive to live. Si Chi's husband was told that Si Chi would have to pay for home study there.

Si Chi never returned to school. By age nineteen, she had four children. The oldest was three. She did not drive until she was nineteen. She never worked outside the home. Her communication with the outside world was limited to the television, guests who came into her home, shopping expeditions, visits with her sisters-in-law, and a weekly class set up by a former missionary to teach practical and biblical English. She is a good mother. She is intelligent, but she is barely able to speak English and unable to function outside the home without assistance from her husband or someone else.

Si Chi's role models are women who are married and producing families. She does not know any educated Hmong women who could serve as alternative role models. Si Chi cannot turn to her mother for guidance, or even to her older sisters or sisters-in-law. Si Chi saw no contradiction between wanting more children immediately and wanting more education. For her, having children is the essence of being Hmong, and having an education is the essence of being American. She is both. Yet she was unable to have both, because the school system and her family did not support her in this endeavor.

1

The Asian American
Academic Success Myth

Why has Asian American academic success emerged as a topic of concern in educational reform in the 1990s? The fundamental answer is economic. It is in the vested interests of those who want to avoid the costs of educational reform to maintain the "success" of Asian Americans as evidence that ethnic minorities can succeed in the existing schools without affirmative action, in-service teacher education, or special program support. Particularly in times of economic recession, the costs and benefits of educating distinct groups, and immigrants in particular, become a political issue.

Among the mixed messages that emerge from the Asian American academic success story is one that involves the age-old debate between nature and nurture, heredity and environment. Is academic achievement the result of innate ability? Or is the ability to achieve in school culturally developed and honed in the home? Are Asian Americans genetically superior in intelligence to European, African, Native, and Latino Americans? Or is the academic success of Asian Americans limited to certain subject areas, in which success is the result of hard work and diligence? Is the success of Asian Americans a result of biological factors, home background, a school system that responds well to the home background, or a home culture that hones academic skills? And what, in fact, is academic success? Whatever it is, it is commonly believed that Asian Americans have it, and African Americans, Latinos, and Native Americans do not. This belief is even less palatable when academic success is equated with intelligence test scores (Jensen, 1969; Herrnstein and Murray, 1994; Itzkoff, 1994). Because there is no conclusion to the nature/nurture debate, no clear definition of intelligence, and no clarity about what standardized I.Q. tests really measure, there can be no clear answers in the debate that is raging over Asian American academic success.

The assumption that Asian Americans are more academically successful than other ethnic minorities appears to echo historical explanations for why African Americans tend to perform less well academically than European Americans. In the 1960s, the deficit theory argued that many African Americans were deprived in their homes due to poverty and the lack of educated role models. Head Start and other programs were designed to offset the problems of inadequate home preparation for school. In turn, it was argued by Jensen (1969), and others more recently (Herrnstein and Murray, 1994), that such compensatory programs are a waste of time because European Americans are genetically superior to African Americans in intelligence. In 1969, Jerome Kagan joined a number of other psychologists to challenge Jensen's work in a discussion entitled "How Much Can We Boost IQ and Scholastic Achievement?" in the *Harvard Educational Review*. Twenty-five years later, however, Kagan wrote, "Some social scientists will also resist acknowledging the contribution of brain chemistry and physiology to behavior because they will worry that, if they let the camel's nose under the tent, the animal will soon be inside, forcing all the residents to leave" (Kagan, 1994).

In the 1980s, anthropologists entered the debate over the comparative performance of ethnic groups in American schools. They rejected the deficit and genetic theories as racist, and instead shifted the attention to teachers and their failure to understand cultural differences in communication style, language usage, and norms of behavior (Erickson, 1987). Ogbu (1978, 1987) argued that while culture, language, and opportunities are important variables, it is more important to look at a group's general economic history and experience of racism in the job market. For Ogbu, this explained the oppositional behavior of many African American youngsters in American schools, and why the average Asian American student performs better academically than the average African American student.

In the early 1990s, the genetics argument reemerged, fueled in part by a lingering economic recession and by growing anti-immigrant sentiments. Itzkoff (1994) blamed the deterioration of the American economy on the decline of national intelligence levels as a result of high fertility rates among poor women, many of whom are immigrants or members of minority groups. Specifically, Itzkoff explained the loss of much of the U.S. automotive market on the decline in intellect among American workers and administrators; but the U.S. automotive industry had lost its competitive edge in the early 1970s, primarily because of the rise in the price of oil, and because of the failure of corporate executives to foresee and meet the need for smaller, more fuel efficient cars.

There is a growing consensus that determinations of intelligence reflect both genetics and environment in combination with a number of other variables, such as cultural norms of behavior, the use of language, and how intelligence is measured. According to an editorial in *The New York Times*, "Put nature and nurture on the scales of science's analytical balance and it becomes a seesaw that never comes to rest. . . . The only lasting resolution to the nature-nurture dispute would come with a deeper understanding of the neurological basis of intelligence. We can measure I.Q. or Scholastic Aptitude Test scores and pretend that the numbers are as meaningful as the horsepower of an engine. The problem is that, for all the successes of neuroscience, we still know so little about what goes on under the cerebral hood" (Johnson, 1994).

The debate about why certain groups tend to succeed in school while others do not has shifted in the last thirty years, from blaming home background to blaming genetics to blaming teachers to blaming history and back to blaming genetics. Now, as a perverse result of the Asian American academic success story, the blame appears to have shifted once again, this time to blaming the students themselves. The implication is that if Asian American students can succeed in the American public schools, then the fault for any particular student's failure lies not with the schools but with the student, whether due to genetics, the home environment, or both. The problem would appear to be one primarily of motivation; the Prologue, however, presented a case study that raised questions about the degree to which motivation really matters when it comes to cultural priorities and the response of schools to non-European cultures.

The Media Portrayal

The mixed messages implicit in the Asian American academic success story have been delivered to the public in a number of ways. In 1987, the *60 Minutes* television show presented "a glowing report" of Asian students' "stunning achievements in the academy" (Takaki, 1989, p. 474). Reporter host Mike Wallace posed the key question that bothers educators who work with minority students in the United States: "Why are Asian Americans doing so exceptionally well in school?" The implied subquestion was, Why are Asian students doing better in school than students who are classified as African, Latino, Native, or European Americans? Wallace remarked: "They must be doing something right. Let's bottle it" (Takaki, 1989, p. 474).

The little-known background of this event was that *60 Minutes* had sent a preparation team to Boulder High School in Colorado to focus part of their program on the Asian American students there. By the end of the visit the school was informed that *60 Minutes* would not be using their school (Donna Lester, Boulder High School, interview with author, June 15, 1987). The Asian American students in Boulder at the time, primarily Hmong and Cambodian refugees from Southeast Asia, were not academically successful, as measured by traditional standards—that is, they did not have high test scores and a high rate of acceptance to elite universities. That Boulder High School graduated a teenage Hmong mother of three who had worked while attending school (along with several other young Hmong mothers), and that she planned to go to college to become one of the first certified Hmong women teachers in the United States, was not regarded as worthy of 60 Minutes attention, because teenage mothers did not fit the image of Asian American academic success.

The story that Wallace was promoting fits the popular image of Asian students that appeared in the 1980s in such major journals as Time, Newsweek, U.S. News and World Report, Fortune, The New Republic, The Christian Science Monitor, and The New York Times. The titles of articles on the subject tell much of the story: "Amazing Asians: The Secret of their Academic Success" (Roberts, 1985); "Asian-Americans: The Soaring Minority" (Dillin, 1985); "Why Asians are Going to the Head of the Class" (Butterfield, 1986); "The Triumph of Asian-Americans" (1985); and "The New Whiz Kids: Why Asian Americans Are Doing So Well, and What it Costs Them" (Brand, 1987). What was not mentioned in these reports is how the Asian students presented were carefully selected. Because popular accounts only told part of the story, the academic success of some Asian American students took on mythical proportions, obscuring the struggle and ultimate failure of others.

There is a fundamental contradiction between the Asian American academic success story and Si Chi's story told in the prologue. It could be argued that Si Chi is a member of a small minority group within the Asian American community; but that minority group, the Hmong, already numbers over 125,000, and most live in concentrated enclaves in California. Numerous other cultural groups are also included in the Asian American ethnic category. Because of their high rate of fertility and immigration, these are among the fastest-growing populations in the United States. Their impact is particularly pronounced in California.

The Academic Basis of the Amazing
Asian American Success Story

Academic writing has portrayed the success of Asian American students as a myth (Chun, 1980; Rigdon, 1991), an image (Hurh and Kim, 1989), and a model for others (Daniels, 1988). Studies of Asian success are generally based on statistics derived from the U.S. Census, standardized test scores, and college acceptance rates, and while overall these statistics do on average paint a positive picture, several academic studies agree that the very category "Asian" is probably invalid (Lai and others, 1990; Lee, 1993; Mizokawa, 1992). Nevertheless, little research has been aimed at the differences that exist among Asian American groups, or at the differences within such groups, including gender differences (Ryckman and Mizokawa, 1990; Mizokawa and Ryckman, 1990; Brandon, 1990). Specifically, there is a fundamental difference in academic achievement between recent immigrants and refugees and Asian Americans whose ancestors crossed the Pacific generations ago. Similar striking differences also exist along class and cultural lines among the great number of Asians who have come to the United States since 1965. It is important to note, for example, that a great difference in academic achievement exists between immigrants and refugees from oral cultures and those who came to the United States from middle-class urban backgrounds in their former home countries. Available studies indicate that there is a fairly reliable correlation between academic success and family educational background.

Most research reports fail to mention the problems with the "Asian American" category itself, simply telling us that Asian American adults are better educated than European Americans. According to the March 1991 census of U.S. residents age twenty-five years and older who trace their ancestry to Asia, 16 percent had at least one year of graduate study, compared to only 9 percent of those who identified themselves as white. (The census and other data sources generally refer to people of European origin as whites).

This census survey only compared adults in the Asian and white categories. A total of 39 percent of Asian American adults had completed four years of college, compared to only 22 percent of white Americans. A total of 82 percent of Asian Americans had graduated from high school, compared to 80 percent of white Americans.

The most significant finding, perhaps, of the 1991 census report was that women who identified themselves as Asian American earned higher salaries than those who identified themselves as white, and that this was especially true for professional women. Asian professional women earned an average of $36,891, compared to white professional women, who earned an average of $29,831. In fact, the image of professional Asian American women as strong competitors is so pervasive that even low-income Mien and Lao students at Richmond High School in California readily agreed that Asian American women earn more than white women. Yet, not a single student raised a hand when asked how many of their own mothers, aunts, grandmothers, or sisters, or any other women in their families, had earned even the $29,150 salary reported as average for all Asian American women, never mind the average of $36,891 reported for Asian American professional women. In reality, the average refugee woman age thirty or older from the mountains of Laos has had less than 1.5 years of formal education (Rumbaut and Weeks, 1986). The statement that Asian American women earn more than American white women is a complete distortion of the reality faced by most of the young people from these Asian cultures.

The 1988 report of the National Educational Longitudinal Study (NELS), which studied the same students every two years from elementary through secondary school, found that more than three-quarters of all those who identified themselves as South Asian, Korean, and Japanese came from families in the upper half of the socioeconomic scale. The same study found that almost as many Southeast Asians and more than half of the self-identified Pacific Islanders came from the lower half. The NELS data, however, does not include Limited English Proficient (LEP) students. Because it is a longitudinal study that predates the arrival of many Southeast Asian students, those included were probably part of the first wave of refugees, the elite in their countries of origin. It is not surprising then that this study found that "all Asian-Americans, with the exception of Pacific Islanders, had above-average educational expectations for their children, and all Asian-Americans, except for Pacific Islanders and Southeast Asians were found to have more learning materials in their homes than other racial and ethnic minorities" (National Educational Longitudinal Study, 1991).

A number of academic studies suggest that some Asian American children have academic advantages over others because of the educational backgrounds of their parents and other family members. Yet, in general, little research attention has been directed at issues of class background, and the influence of family educational background has consistently been undervalued. For example, a study by Caplan, Whitmore, Bui, and Trautman (1985) drew public attention by claiming that even children of "boat" refugees fit the image of the successful Asian student (see also Caplan, Whitmore, and Choy, 1989; Caplan, Choy, and Whitmore, 1991). The public image of this group was that they were extremely poor, adrift between countries with nothing but the clothes on their backs; but, in reality, in the aftermath of the various wars fought in Southeast Asia through 1970, "boat people" from Vietnam were not the poorest of refugees. They may have been brutalized in their escape, but unlike the refugees who walked across Cambodia, or swam across the Mekong River from Laos to Thailand, their backgrounds afforded them the ability to pay for passage. Their backgrounds also often afforded them a tradition of high levels of education. What the Caplan, Whitmore, Bui, and Trautman (1985) study really tells us is that students from well-educated backgrounds succeed academically regardless of their status as refugees.

A less-noted finding of the Caplan, Whitmore, Bui, and Trautman study was the strong relationship between student achievement and family background. Not only were the parents of academically successful children well educated, but so were their grandparents. "Parents of children who excel in school . . . are more likely to have come from urban backgrounds and to have had parents who themselves were comparatively better educated" (1985, p. 5). Similarly, Lai and others (1990) found a strong link between parents' education and socioeconomic status and student achievement on standardized tests in a study that included Cambodian and Hmong students. In a 1987 study in San Diego, Rumbaut and Ima found that the standardized reading scores of Hmong students whose parents had more than six years of education were more than 100 percent higher than the scores of students whose parents had less education.

Measuring Academic Success

Data from the Rumbaut and Ima study was particularly provocative within the debate about academic success. In particular, it raised the issue of what academic success is and how it should be measured. The authors regarded the Hmong as academically successful because of their surprisingly high grade point averages. Nevertheless, the study also found that Hmong students tested poorly on standardized tests. This suggests a discrepancy between what is perceived as academic success and real academic achievement—or more to the point, between what Hmong students were being taught and what was evaluated on the standardized tests.

The study found that 40 percent of the Hmong students had grade point averages above 3.0, and that the Hmong had the smallest percentage of students with grade point averages below 2.0 of any group in the city. Yet, the Hmong averaged the lowest score for reading comprehension on the Comprehensive Tests of Basic Skills (CTBS) of any Southeast Asian group. Hmong students also scored abysmally low on reading vocabulary and all other reading tests. Grades are, of course, a subjective measure of achievement, and often reflect effort and neatness. In other words, attentiveness and good behavior pay off in terms of grades, and it does not hurt the Hmong that their teachers often say they "love" them. Teachers generally concur that Southeast Asian refugee students are model pupils. "They are quieter, more polite and respectful than other minority students. They do their homework and are eager learners," one teacher explained to me. Another said, "Teachers almost fight to get them in their rooms, they want them in their rooms so bad." An elementary school principal told me, "[Hmong students] are out-shining our American children. When they are integrated into reg-ular classrooms with American-born whites and American-born blacks, they [are the best students]. They're surpassing them in every area: math, language, reading, everything, particularly math. If you watch them after they are integrated in a regular classroom—you're not really looking for it, you just walk into a classroom—the Asian child will pick up a book and read. The American child will go to the corner and play." Teachers who have had Hmong students agree that the Hmong have more discipline in the use of their free time. The same principal said to me, "The Southeast Asians are the most motivated of all to learn, more so than our American children. They very rarely don't do homework."

Most often high averages on standardized mathematics tests are held up as proof of the academic superiority of Asian American stu-dents. It is widely believed that mathematics is one area in which Asian American students excel. Yet, Tsang (1988) found that little actual scholarship has focused on breaking out the mathematics achievement of different Asian American groups, for two reasons. One is that the number of different Asian American groups has been considered too small to justify separate statistical analyses; the other is the assumption that since all Asian American students are doing so well in mathematics, no research is necessary. In fact, Tsang found that "although there is a higher proportion of Asian-American students who are high math achievers, there is also a larger proportion who are low math achievers. The mean scores only provide us with a generalization and do not reflect the diverse achievement levels of Asian-American students" (p. 127).

In 1988, for the first time, special funding was made available to analyze the California Assessment Program (CAP) scores in terms of specific Asian and Pacific Islander ethnic groups. The groups that Lai and others (1990) analyzed included students who had identified themselves as Asian Indian, Cambodian, Chinese, Filipino, Hmong, Japanese, Korean, Laotian, Pacific Islander, and Vietnamese. In a paper presented at the annual meeting of the American Educational Research Association in April 1990, Lai and others concluded:

> This study verified emphatically that California API [Asian and Pacific Islander] eighth-grade students are extremely diverse in their Reading and Written Expression performance, which is related to variables such as ethnic-group membership, generation in the U.S., English fluency, and which skills area is being measured. So diverse were the mean performances that we suggest that writers who use phrases such as the "performance of Asian (or Asian American) students was . . ." are probably guilty of unwarranted stereotyping. Furthermore, we suggest that it is even generally inappropriate to refer to the "achievement of Chinese American (nonimmigrant) students," for example, without taking into account factors such as generation in the U.S., parents' education, or amount of time spent on homework each workday.

Many of the students categorized as Asian American are either immigrants or children of immigrants who came from countries that have very competitive educational systems (Tsang, 1988). Teachers in Asian countries often focus their energies on preparing their students to test well, particularly in mathematics, in order for them to gain entrance to higher levels of learning. Consequently, these students may come to U.S. schools with highly developed testing skills. This is certainly not true, however, of all students of Asian ancestry, as the Hmong case study in Chapter Three will demonstrate.

Studies that conclude that Asian Americans are better educated than European Americans, such as the March 1991 census survey discussed earlier, may have a backlash effect. For example, they imply that European American students' access to higher education must be protected from Asian American students with university quotas. In recent years, major research universities, such as Harvard University, University of California at Los Angeles, and the University of California at Berkeley, have been charged with setting admissions quotas for Asian Americans to prevent "overrepresentation" of people who fall into this category. A compliance review of Harvard University by the U.S. Department of Education's Office of Civil Rights, made public in 1990, found that "over the last ten years Asian American applicants have been admitted at a significantly lower rate than white applicants; however, . . . the primary cause of the disparity was the preference given to children of alumni and recruited athletes and that [the preferences] were legitimate and not a pretext for discrimination" (U.S. Commission on Civil Rights, 1992). The Harvard argument in favor of recruiting athletes and the children of alumni resembles the argument used in the U.S. 1924 Immigration Act, which restricted annual immigration to 2 percent of the size of the population from each country that existed in the United States in 1890, resulting in the restriction of immigration from southern Europe and Japan. The Harvard policy resulted in limiting the access of ethnic groups such as Asian Americans, who do not have a large number of alumni parents or outstanding athletes in a large variety of sports.

Hirano-Nakanishi (1992) found that the percentage of California high school graduates identifying themselves as Asian or Pacific Islanders who were eligible for entrance into the California State University system increased from 49 percent in 1983 to 60 percent in 1990. More than two-thirds of Asian and Pacific Islander high school graduates had taken college preparation classes. Yet, the average verbal score on SATs of Asian and Pacific Islanders were the lowest of any racial group. Hirano-Nakanishi also found that the majority were classified as Limited English Proficient at entry. Only 11 percent of Asian and Pacific Islander high school graduates who attended California State University campuses in 1990 were placed in regular classes.

The Impact of Poverty

Kan and Liu (1986) concluded from their study of Asian Americans that the high achievement of Asian American children in schools could be explained in part by the fact that "most Asian children come from highly educated families with considerable resources for children to become familiar with educational tools, such as computer terminals at home" (p. 24). Not only do the Hmong not have highly educated families, but Hmong families are less likely than other Asian immigrant groups to have such resources as home computers, chiefly because they have had less education and are poorer than other Asian immigrants or other refugee groups.

The Rumbaut and Weeks (1986) study found that 94 percent of the Hmong in San Diego lived below the poverty level. The majority of Cambodians, ethnic Lao, and Chinese Vietnamese also lived below the poverty level, but fewer Vietnamese were below the poverty level than any other refugee groups. By comparison, less than one-sixth of the total Asian immigrant population lived in poverty.

Kan and Liu (1986) argued that there was a "waiting period" from the date of immigration to when immigrants rise above the poverty level. In almost every Asian immigrant group, the percentage of families with school-age children below the poverty level declined the longer the groups were in the United States. The exception worth noting was the high percentages of Filipino and Asian Indians born here who live below the poverty level. The waiting period may also not apply to Asian refugees who do not have the educational backgrounds to move into higher occupational positions as they learn more English.

Immigrant Rigor, or Is It Vigor?

Academic advantages are only one side of the story of academic success. Kan and Liu (1986) suggested that many Asian immigrants are academically successful because of their "immigrant rigor." Immigrant rigor is the incentive that children gain from knowing that their families were rich or powerful in their first country and are now poor and powerless in the United States. Kan and Liu found that the successes of fellow immigrants inspired immigrant rigor. I prefer to call this characteristic "vigor," because an incentive often accompanies the beginning of a new life and tends to carry a more positive energy than "rigor."

Hmong students appear to have a tremendous amount of immigrant vigor; they are highly motivated despite extreme poverty, uneducated parents, and having few Hmong role models who have achieved financial or academic success. It seems that, for the Hmong, immigrant vigor reflects their cultural priority of survival. The fact that some recent immigrants and refugees do have successful role models suggests that certain class advantages have been carried from their country of origin. As with earlier immigrants at the turn of the century (Perlmann, 1988), "the class position of an ethnic group in the American social structure was itself a result of the premigration characteristics of the group, and of the extent of discrimination against it, as well as of employment opportunities in the particular economy."

Approximately 31 percent of the Vietnamese, Chinese Vietnamese, and ethnic Lao included in a national study in the early 1980s listed their former occupation in Asia as "students" (Caplan, Whitmore, Bui, and Trautman, 1985). Ethnic Vietnamese had higher-status occupations in their country of origin than did ethnic Lao or Chinese Vietnamese, including 11 percent professionals (doctors, architects, professors, and judges), and 4 percent military officers (Caplan, Whitmore, Bui, and Trautman, 1985). The ethnic Lao had fewer professionals and fewer officers. Characteristic of Chinese elsewhere in Southeast Asia, Chinese Vietnamese reported

fewer professional positions and very few military positions compared to the Vietnamese, but there were more managers among
Chinese Vietnamese than among any other refugee group. These
are the role models by which these immigrants could set their sights.

Given that until recently education was a novelty for the
majority of Hmong, their role models are much different than
those of other Asian immigrants. In particular, there are almost no
educated Hmong women to act as role models. Almost all the
women role models for teenage Hmong girls are married and producing families. Hmong girls who continue to study beyond
puberty are exceptional.

The flexibility of the Hmong culture is revealed in their learning to adapt their male role models and cultural expectations in
order to survive. Micah Vang, a Hmong scholar, noted that Hmong
role models and cultural expectations for males have changed several times in his lifetime. They have been adapted first to conditions
of isolation, then to war and displacement, and finally to life in an
industrial, consumer society. Male role models changed first from
farmers to soldiers when the Southeast Asia war spread to Laos in
the 1960s, then from soldiers to scholars in the early 1970s when
some Hmong returned to their families from schools in Vientiane
and France; and as the Hmong came down to the lowlands from the
mountains and began to realize that they had been involved in a
war of technology between the superpowers, they began to regard
education as their handle on the future.

There is thus a great flaw in much academic writing about Asian
Americans. When the differences among Asians are explored, key
discrepancies in family educational background and class advantage
emerge. The data suggest that children with educated parents and
professional role models have a head start over children with preliterate parents. The studies by Kan and Liu (1986), Rumbaut and
Ima (1987), and Caplan, Bui, Whitmore, and Trautman (1985)
have all shown that academic achievement correlates with family
education levels and the presence of educational resources in the
home. Hmong role models are not professional but military or

domestic. Given these limitations there is little reason to expect that the Hmong will move into a higher professional class after a waiting period.

Perlmann's (1988) theory that certain class advantages are carried over from the country of origin to the country of resettlement compliments Kan and Liu's (1986) theory that home, family and community role models influence the success of Asian American students. Students from well-off immigrant families, or children of formerly rich refugees, tend to have higher levels of education. Although Perlmann's theory was based on turn-of-the-century immigrants to Providence, Rhode Island, it fits the case of today's Asian refugees and immigrants as well. Contemporary Asian immigrants who have high levels of education or who had professional positions in their first countries probably have children who study hard and do well academically, at least in part to help their family return to its previous class status.

New Stereotypes, Old Problems

The amazing Asian American success story appears to be a new form of racism, which may be defined as any form of bigotry that contributes to racial intimidation and violence. Popular acceptance of generic images of Asian American success owes much to the treatment of Asians by U.S. media. A 1992 report by the U.S. Commission on Civil Rights, entitled "Civil Rights Issues Facing Asian Americans in the 1990s," put the problem in the following terms:

> Asian Americans are seldom the focus of news media coverage. When the news media do portray Asian Americans, they often treat them in a superficial, stereotypical fashion. For instance, a common focus of the stories about Asian Americans is the success of some immigrants and refugees who arrived in the United

States with nothing, overcame all barriers, and achieved high levels of education and income. At the same time, the news media almost never cover other aspects of Asian American communities, such as poverty or the problems of limited-English-proficient youngsters. Thus, the news media have played a role in disseminating the "model minority" stereotype of Asian Americans. [p. 182]

The story of an apparently "successful" minority was not created by racist people to divide minorities; rather, it was simply a story too good to question adequately, particularly at a time when affirmative action was being questioned. Good stories sell, and for the private news industry, profit is the bottom line; but such critical neglect (illustrated by the 60 *Minutes* anecdote told earlier in this chapter) hints at a new kind of racial stereotyping that blocks greater awareness of the diversity of Asian cultures and the complex pressures on young Asian Americans.

Of course, the media should not shoulder all the blame. Much of what the media reports is influenced one way or another by what the public wants to believe. This seems to be the case in regard to African American and Latino students, who are stereotyped as unsuccessful, and it would seem to be true that some people want to believe that Asian American students can be more successful at the same schools with the same resources as other minority groups. This perspective shifts the responsibility for the high rate of minority-student failure from the schools—and hence the taxpayers—to the students themselves and their families. The model-minority myth also supports those who would eliminate affirmative action.

The amazing Asian American success story is a double-edged sword in its impact on Asian American welfare. The perception of Asian American academic success is now so widespread that Asian Americans are not considered minorities in need of affirmative action. As a result, school administrators at all levels do not keep careful statistics on Asian American students. Due to the Asian

American success story and the failure to analyze existing data carefully, Asian Americans are not regarded as "at-risk" students—regardless of the reality of their situations. In schools I visited throughout the country I was commonly told that "the Asians are such good students." Because of this widespread attitude, many schools do not examine, or in some cases even notice, discrepancies between high grade point averages and low standardized-test scores. Many schools do not monitor or even record the dropout rates among Asian Americans. The result is that some school districts do not realize, for example, that they are losing as many as half their female Hmong students before graduation. School districts also have not recognized the special counseling needs of students from other countries until after those students have dropped out of school.

Widespread acceptance of the Asian American academic success story hints at discrimination; it is an excuse not to undertake the difficult task of reforming U.S. schools to help students understand and value a multicultural society. The attitude that "We do not need to worry about them because they do so well" is divisive and destructive. The reality is that recent immigrants and refugees from Southeast Asia, China, the Philippines, and the Pacific Islands require the same special attention that any member of a cultural minority in America requires.

In this chapter I have told a story of distortion and misrepresentation, of how popular stereotypes are inaccurate and damaging. In the next chapter, I turn to explaining who Asian Americans are and how the demographics of this group have changed dramatically in the last twenty years because of changes in patterns of immigration to the United States.

The New Asian Americans

This chapter provides a brief history of Asian American immigration and some basic background on the cultural and linguistic distinctions between Asian Americans. It introduces the major Southeast Asian groups that constitute a large segment of the contemporary Asian American community: Hmong, Mien, ethnic Lao, ethnic Vietnamese, Chinese Vietnamese, Amer-Asians, and Cambodians. The purpose of this introduction is not to provide a stereotypical description of each of the above groups, but to help the reader to distinguish the Hmong, who will become a major focus of the book, from the other groups and to understand why each group should be regarded distinctly, rather than as simply "Asian American" or "Southeast Asian."

Efforts to generalize inevitably lead to racial stereotyping, no matter how sensitive the approach, because they simplify and thereby trivialize culture; but, as will be shown in the next chapter, statistics indicate that reliable differences in academic achievement can be found by distinguishing students according to such characteristics as gender, rural or urban origin, parents' socioeconomic class, parents' educational levels, or immigration history (multigenerational American, undocumented alien, recent immigrant, or refugee). One must always recognize that such information is, however, only general and not directly relevant to individuals.

In Laos alone there are sixty different ethnic groups speaking eighty-five different languages (Tayanin and Vang, 1992, p. 10; Grimes, 1988). Mainland Southeast Asia also includes Cambodia, Vietnam, Thailand, and Myanmar (formerly Burma). Insular Southeast Asia includes Indonesia, the Philippines, Brunei, Malaysia, and Singapore. Both within and among these countries there are broad distinctions in culture, language, history, and educational background. It is dangerous to generalize about such diversity, because human beings and their cultures are innately dynamic entities.

Asians: An Invalid Category

A general consensus exists among those academic researchers who focus on Asian and Pacific American students that so great are the differences among Asians that any reference to "Asian American" is incorrect stereotyping (Mizokawa and Ryckman, 1990; Ryckman and Mizokawa, 1990; Lai and others, 1990). As Mizokawa (1992, p. 2) wrote, "The problem with this designation—'Asian Americans'—is that it encompasses so many different peoples as to be rendered virtually meaningless." He further explained, "The Asians range from the Caucasoid stock of the Ainu of Japan and the Spanish colonials through the Mongolian ancestries of the people of China, Japan, and Korea, to the Malaysian, Melanesian, Micronesian and Polynesian mixtures in the Pacific Basin."

In her introduction to *Asian American Experiences in the United States*, Lee (1993) wrote, "In the totality of American perception, all Asians are somehow lumped together into one racial group." One might add to this that it is particularly inappropriate to lump together Southeast Asians of rural backgrounds (Hmong and Mien mountain people and certain Lao and Cambodian refugees) with Japanese, Indian, Korean, Chinese, or Filipino immigrants, or even urban refugees from Vietnam, many of whom have highly educated families. Additionally, few studies and most statistical information fail to distinguish the great number of elite students who are visiting the United States—from Japan, Korea, and elsewhere—from Asian Americans who were born here or live here permanently. Some scholars argue that Asians in general share more in terms of cultural values with each other than they do with people from European backgrounds. While this may be true in the case of certain cultures, its relevance is clearly stretched in comparing the education of people from the mountains of Laos with highly educated students from Tokyo. Think, for example, how erroneous it might have seemed in the early 1900s to have lumped together all European immigrants to America's shores. (Most English still do not consider themselves European, despite the 1991 Maastricht treaty that essentially includes England in a single European body of law and economy.) Yet, the differences among Asian immigrants today are, if anything, greater than the differences among Europeans in the early twentieth century.

To show how dangerous general categorical classifications can be, when I began in 1986 to research the education of Southeast Asians in a New England city that I will call Milltown, the Superintendent's office informed me that there were no Asians in their schools. I knew to the contrary that Hmong students had been in their schools for eight years, because I had been living there when they first arrived, and I wondered why there was no statistical record of them. Through the state's department of education I later discovered that Milltown had classified all Hmong, Lao, Cambodian, and other Southeast Asians as Pacific Islanders. Pacific Islanders generally include people from the Samoan, Fijian, Tongan, Solomon, and other islands in the Pacific Ocean. When I pointed out the error to the person in charge of the data, she asked, "Aren't Asians and Pacific Islanders the same thing?"

Early Asian Americans

Early Asian Americans include, but are not limited to, those whose ancestors came from Japan, the Philippines, China, Hong Kong, Taiwan, Malaysia, India, and Korea. Like most immigrants, the earliest immigrants from Asia came to the United States to work. Asian laborers expanded railroads throughout the west. Many early Chinese immigrants to California were miners, coming to mine the mountain of gold (Chan, 1986). Others worked in construction and agriculture. Still others came as students to study in American universities and colleges. Overall, however, the history of Asian immigration prior to 1850 is sketchy. We have no idea how many immigrants came across the Pacific, because national statistics only recorded arrivals at ports on the East Coast and the Gulf of Mexico. Between 1854 and 1883, however, it is estimated that three hundred thousand newcomers arrived from southern China alone (Arnold, Minocha, and Fawcett, 1987). Initially, the Chinese were welcomed as a source of cheap labor to counter the East Coast challenge to develop overseas markets.

Immigrants were drawn to the United States from across the Pacific by the same magnet that attracted people from across the Atlantic: the promise of work and hope for a better future. The onset of the industrial revolution in the United States created jobs, wealth, and the hope for a better life; but the industrial revolution also displaced workers and created unemployment. In the 1880s, unions that had been created in the second half of the nineteenth century to protect workers reacted to the nation's first period of widespread unemployment by, among other things, blaming Chinese immigrants because they worked for lower wages than Europeans and were not union members (Takaki, 1989, pp. 10–11; U.S. Commission on Civil Rights, 1992, p. 6). This reaction led to the Chinese Exclusion Act of 1882. The Act marked the advent of a period of extreme anti-Asian sentiment. In the years that followed it was reinforced by other racist policies.

The Chinese Exclusion Act was the first of two great watersheds in Asian American immigration history. It forbade immigration from China for ten years. In 1892 the Geary Act extended the immigration ban on the Chinese and required Chinese Americans to carry "certificates of residence" (U.S. Commission on Civil

Rights, 1992, p. 3). The identification cards that some politicians are currently calling for immigrants to carry to prove they are legal residents are equivalent to these certificates. The Chinese Exclusion Act also prevented Chinese in the United States from obtaining naturalized citizenship, even though the Fourteenth Amendment of 1870 granted citizenship to all children who were born here (Arnold, Minocha, and Fawcett, 1987, p. 10). Again, a contemporary equivalent to this prohibition was the effort in California in the 1990s to deny citizenship to children born in the United States if they are born to a parent who does not have proper immigration documents. In 1922, the Supreme Court ruled that the Japanese were also barred from naturalized citizenship (*Cozawa* v. *United States* 260 U.S. 178 [1922]); and in 1923, in *U.S.* v. *Bhagwat Singh Thind*, the Supreme Court barred East Indians from naturalized citizenship, reversing two prior decisions, by ruling that the term "white" did not include all Caucasians (Takaki, 1989, p. 299).

Such efforts to reduce or eliminate the growth in the Asian population in the United States ran into trouble, however, when it came to Filipinos. For forty years following its seizure in the Spanish American War, the Philippines was a territory of the United States, and therefore Filipinos were technically American citizens. In 1930, the first year that population statistics were kept, there were more than one hundred thousand Filipinos in the United States, primarily in California and Hawaii (Carino, 1987). Nevertheless, the Tydings-McDuffie Act of 1934 specifically limited the total number of Filipino immigrants to fifty per year.

Racist U.S. immigration policies were not limited to periods of unemployment. The 1922 Cable Act stated that any woman who married an "alien ineligible to citizenship shall cease to be a citizen of the U.S." (Takaki, 1989, p. 15); and the National Origins Act of 1924, which limited immigration from any country outside of North America to 2 percent of the 1890 population and was intended to limit immigration from southern and eastern Europe, effectively reduced Asian immigration from almost twenty thousand in 1924 to thirty-five hundred in 1925 (Arnold, Minocha, and Fawcett, 1987, p.10). This act strongly affected Japanese immigrants, who had been recruited as a source of labor in the aftermath of the Chinese Exclusion Act. The 1924 Act also forbade women from China, Japan, Korea, and India from entering the United States, even as wives of U.S. citizens, in order to limit the number of native-born Asian American citizens. There was no limit on European wives (Takaki, 1989, p. 14). This law was not changed until the 1945 War Brides Act permitted the immigration of Asian spouses and children of U.S. servicemen. The McCarran-Walter Act of 1952 allowed Asians to become naturalized citizens. The law barring Asian immigrants from naturalized citizenship was rescinded only after China became a World War II ally of the United States, and after the sons of many East Indian, Filipino, and Japanese immigrants had fought and died in the service of U.S. military forces (Takaki, 1989, p. 413).

Family Reunification and the 1965 Immigration Act

The second great watershed in Asian immigration to the United States was the 1965 Immigration Act. Among other consequences, this policy abolished National Origins quotas. Immigrants were now allowed to enter as immediate family members of U.S. citizens, or according to a preference system by which a limited number of spaces were allocated to necessary occupations and skills, but family reunification was given great priority. The number of immigrants qualifying under the preference system was initially limited to twenty thousand per country per year; no limits were set, however, on the total number of parents, spouses, and unmarried minor children of U.S. citizens who could enter the United States. This system opened the door to great numbers of immigrants who could now avoid all quota barriers. As a result of the family reunification priority, the number of immigrants from Asian countries soared. In 1960, none of the ten countries sending the largest number of immigrants to the U.S. were Asian; by 1985, four of the five largest sending countries were Asian (Arnold, Minocha, and Fawcett, 1987, p. 111). The Philippine islands alone have sent more immigrants to the United States since 1960 than any country except Mexico (Arnold, Minocha, and Fawcett, 1987, p. 114). Since the mid 1970s, the majority of Asian immigrants have come to the United States on family reunification visas.

Initially, the 1965 Act worked well, considering its goals. During the 1960s and early 1970s the majority of Asian immigrants who entered the United States were given priority because of their occupations and high levels of particular skills. As a result, a new profile of the Asian immigrant emerged, that of the student or well-educated professional. Many of these immigrants first came as college students; some later adjusted their status to that of permanent resident. Many came from upper-income families that afforded them the opportunity to study English in their country of origin before attending a university in the United States.

After 1980, the unlimited provision for reunification of immediate family members began to take hold. The professionals who came under occupational preferences and the young Asian students who stayed on after completing their degree and became citizens began to bring in immediate family members—their mothers, fathers, spouses, and children. They in turn brought in their own immediate families after becoming American citizens themselves and waiting the required five years. Increasingly, the extended family members came from rural, less-educated backgrounds. Consequently, the profile of Asian immigrants changed.

Refugees of the Southeast Asian War

Following the family reunification provision of the 1965 Immigration Act, the second most-significant event that brought new Asians to the United States was the denouement of the Southeast Asian war. Under the Paris Agreement of 1973, the United States withdrew all troops from and stopped bombing South Vietnam (Hersh, 1983, pp. 561–632). Without U.S. support it was not long before the corrupt regime there crumbled. This withdrawal of troops also meant the withdrawal of U.S. military support for the Hmong army in Laos under General Vang Pao, the Lao army, and the government of Lon Nol in Cambodia, even though there was no cease-fire in place for Laos and Cambodia (Hersh, 1983, p. 561). In theory, the U.S. military was never supposed to have been in Laos or Cambodia, because these countries were designated as neutral by a 1962 agreement between the United States and the Soviet Union (Halberstam, 1972). In reality, the United States had actively supported military forces in Cambodia and Laos for some time; and of course the Soviet Union and China, at different times, were also involved in training and supporting the communist Pathet Lao in Laos and Khmer Rouge in Cambodia.

The withdrawal of U.S. troops and military support created power vacuums in Laos, Cambodia, and Vietnam. Political realignment moved quickly. After North Vietnam took over the south, South Vietnam ceased to exist as a separate country on April 30, 1975. Laos was taken over by the Pathet Lao. Cambodia was taken over by Pol Pot and the Khmer Rouge party, which were then supported by China. As a result of war, political realignment, and havoc in the aftermath of war, more than two million people were displaced, and more than half of them eventually came to the United States as refugees.

According to a statistician of the U.S. Immigration and Naturalization Service (INS), as of May 1992, of the one million refugees from Southeast Asia approximately 100,000 were Hmong and other mountain people from Laos, approximately 125,000 were ethnic Lao, approximately 650,000 were from Vietnam, and approximately 150,000 were Cambodians (Linda Gordon, conversation with the author, Washington, D.C., May 1992). These numbers do not include the large number of Southeast Asians who were sponsored by their relatives who had become U.S. citizens, and those who had entered the United States as immigrants under family reunification preferences without access to the special welfare programs created for refugees, which the INS estimated at 140,000 in 1992. Most of these people were Vietnamese; they included the children of U.S. servicemen, and other Americans who entered as first-priority immigrants. As political relations between the U.S. and Vietnamese governments improve, and as more Vietnamese become U.S. citizens who are eligible to sponsor the immigration of family members, more immigrants can be expected to arrive as a result of family reunification. Furthermore, Rumbaut and Weeks (1986) estimate that high birthrates among Southeast Asian immigrants have increased the size of the Southeast Asian population in the United States by approximately 25 percent since they began arriving here.

Settlement Patterns

Beginning with the earliest arrival of refugees from Southeast Asia in mid 1975, the first resettlement objective of the U.S. Department of State was to scatter Southeast Asians throughout the country so that no one area would be too heavily affected. The plan backfired. As soon as refugees began arriving in the United States, they began networking to find out about a host of factors: the safety of particular communities, the availability of jobs, the weather conditions in different areas, and the relative levels of social services in various parts of the country. Southeast Asian resettlement has since been dominated by large-scale "secondary" migration through which groups have congregated in specific areas of the county. The settlement of the Hmong, for instance, came to be concentrated in a few areas of California, New England, Minnesota, Washington, Colorado, North Carolina, and Wisconsin.

Subsequent immigration has been characterized by family reunification, resulting in newcomers going to areas that already have large communities of Southeast Asians. The U.S. government tried anew to limit the impact by "closing" certain areas to refugee resettlement, but again the Hmong and others defeated federal policy through secondary migration. These migration patterns along with high rates of Hmong fertility have caused the number of Hmong students in particular school districts to escalate dramatically.

Differences Among Southeast Asian Refugees

Initially, the first wave of refugees from the war were similar in many respects to Asian immigrants of the mid 1970s. These early arrivals were primarily from Vietnam; the majority were urban, had worked with Americans, were well educated and well connected. They were the elite. The second wave typically brought lower-level military and government officials, businessmen, and others with connec-tions. They were also educated, and often came from urban areas where they had considerable contact with Americans during the war years. The third wave brought the poorest people, sometimes relatives of previous waves, often farmers and village merchants with little formal education and minimal experience with Western culture and technology. This third wave included great numbers of Hmong, Mien, lowland Lao, and Cambodians.

A fourth wave began arriving in 1986. It consisted of loyalists, die-hards, and those who were unwilling to give up hope of returning to their countries until all other alternatives had failed. They had seen the most of war and spent the longest time in refugee camps. The people of this fourth wave are similar to those of the second wave in that the adults may have had relatively privileged posi-tions in their past (as village chiefs or second-tier military officers); however, having spent many years in refugee camps, they have had greater exposure to Western education and technology. More of their children have attended primary school than in previous waves. They have been internationalized by the camp experience (Walker and Moffat, 1987). Because of the politicized nature of their par-ents' commitment and because of their parents' extensive experi-ence with war and deprivation, the children of the fourth wave are often more politicized than those of earlier waves. The prepared-ness of fourth-wave refugees for life in the United States is a result of the tension between the improvement of educational programs for refugees and the winding down of funding for such programs.

Distinctions among the waves of Southeast Asian immigrants quickly became apparent in the United States. Those who arrived from Cambodia, Laos, and Vietnam prior to 1978 had almost ten years of education on average (Rumbaut and Weeks, 1986). Those who arrived between 1978 and 1983 had an average of about six years of education. The Hmong in the Rumbaut and Weeks study had an average of only 1.6 years of education, the Lao and Cambodians had an average of around five years, the Chinese Vietnamese had 6.7 years, and the Vietnamese had an average of 9.8 years of education. (For comparison's sake, according to the 1980 census whites had an average of 12.5 years of education, Japanese Americans had 12.9 years, Chinese Americans had 13.4 years, and Korean Americans had 13 years.)

I now turn to some important cultural distinctions between specific groups of Southeast Asians who now live in the United States. This is meant as an introduction only, and is by no means a complete description. It is aimed at introducing the origins of some of the challenges that teachers, administrators, and guidance counselors in U.S. schools must meet. Some of the most important of these problems are lack of former schooling, gender roles, and an oral tradition.

The Hmong

Living high in the chimney-steep mountains in the north of the country, the majority of mountain people in Laos were isolated from the industrial-age technology until the war came to Laos. "Being situated in the mountains in remote, isolated villages few, if any, Hmong had any schooling," wrote Vangyi (1980). The home was the basis of informal education for Hmong children, and everyone took part in teaching children the practical and culturally correct ways of existence (Barney, 1967). Education has played a primary role in reshaping the attitudes of the generation of Hmong children who have grown up in the refugee camps (Walker and Moffat, 1986) and in the United States.

Around 1961, when the United States military began recruiting Hmong as fighters, the U.S. Agency for International Development (AID) contracted the University of Hawaii to build primary schools and train teachers for the Hmong (Yang, 1981). The schools' language of instruction was Lao. Many of them were built in the areas to which the Hmong had been relocated so that the U.S. military could bomb their villages to prevent Communist takeovers (Mottin, 1980). AID and the Lao Ministry of Education established two high schools for Hmong in Sam Thong and Ban Nam Mo. AID also provided for a six-month teacher-training program for Hmong who had graduated from primary school (Yang, 1981). After completion of the course, the teachers returned to the new schools that were located in remote villages. Only a few rich Hmong had attended French high schools before this time or attended the *École Supériere de Pédagogie*, a teacher preparation college, in Vientiane, the capital of Laos. Even fewer had been sent to France to study.

In Laos, education for the Hmong, like positions of leadership, was reserved for men. Hmong girls were allowed to attend school, but few did. Even in refugee camps in Thailand there was a great gender imbalance in who attended school, until 1983, when Sister Marie Julian, an American nun, and Father Edward Brady, an American Jesuit priest, improved attendance rates and the gender ratio dramatically for the youngest girls. By 1986, out of approximately eight thousand primary students at Ban Vinai camp, 63 percent of the children age seven to fourteen were in school. Nevertheless, by grade six only 11 percent of the children were girls, because most girls had dropped out (Blanchard and Horn, 1986). Few older girls took the correspondence and private courses offered around the camp.

Women have no official status in the Hmong authority system. A woman's most important roles in the Hmong culture are to form alliances between clans through marriage, and to provide her husband with many children. Her identity is based on her role as wife and mother. Motherhood is not separated from the rest of the Hmong culture, which is inclusive: all spheres are interdependent, and independence or the idea of "self" is immediately suspect. The family, not the individual, is the unit of labor,.

The Hmong are strictly a patriarchal people whose "social system implies certain obligations to their fathers, elder brothers, and leaders" (Dunnigan, 1982). The authority system is hierarchical and based on the family clan. Everyone with the same last name is assumed to be a member of the same clan, whether born into it or through marriage. Clan members refer to one another as "cousins" or "brothers." Marriage within one's own clan is incestuous.

Unlike the majority of Southeast Asian refugees, the Hmong are not Buddhists, and their culture does not include written religious texts. Despite the efforts of missionaries in Laos and the refugee camps of Thailand, few Hmong adopted Christianity in Southeast Asia. Most Hmong believe in ancestor spirits and that the world of spirits interfaces with our world. Shamans serve the important role of intermediaries between the two worlds. A number of Hmong have converted to Christianity in the United States, however.

Hmong culture is based on an oral tradition. Their written language was first formalized in 1952 and 1953 by French and American missionaries using a romanized alphabet (McGinn, 1989). Yang (1992) refers to legends of how the Hmong once had a writing system, but it was destroyed in order to conceal it from the Han Chinese. According to this story, books were thrown into the Yellow River and the characters were integrated into Hmong embroidery and *paj ntaub* (flower cloths). In 1959 in Laos, the Hmong prophet Shong Lue Yang developed a written language for the Hmong based on these characters (Smalley, Vang, and Yang, 1990), "but his writing system has become associated with a religious movement that counters traditional Hmong beliefs" (Yang, 1992).

In lieu of books, Hmong history was committed to memory and passed down orally from father to son, entwined with animistic beliefs, during annual Hmong New Year rituals. Three themes run through Hmong oral history: a person's word is his bond, the Hmong must defend itself against all others, and children must care for their parents. Hmong oral tales explain that the Hmong came from a land of snow and ice, "behind the back of China," where days and nights lasted six months and "the trees were rare and very small, and the people were clothed in furs" (Mottin, 1980, p. 15). Von Eickestedt argued that, based on geographical evidence, the Hmong originally came from the steppe region of Tibet, Mongolia, and old China (Cooper, 1984, p. 262). From there they migrated to China and spread out into Southeast Asia. The existence, however, of numerous other theories about the geographic origins of the Hmong reflects the political schisms in the Hmong leadership (Schein, 1993, p. 36).

Historians agree that most Hmong were in China until around 1810. Today, an estimated 2.2 million Hmong still live in southern China, in Guizhou, Guiyang, Hunan, Sichuan, Guangxi, and Yunnan provinces (Yang, 1992). The Hmong are one of many ethnic minority peoples—including the Mien, Khmu, Tai Dam, and Lahu—who still live in the rugged mountainous areas of southern China. In the United States, the majority of Hmong live in the Central Valley of California. Sizable Hmong communities also exist in other parts of California, and in Minnesota, Rhode Island, Wisconsin, Washington, Colorado, and North Carolina. Smaller communities of Hmong exist in just about every state.

The Hmong now living in the United States are all of the branches of the tribe that migrated into Laos. Hmong legend says that there were seven branches in China: Blue Hmong, White Hmong, Striped Hmong, Black Hmong, Chinese Hmong, Chee Hmong, and Chue Hmong. The three major branches of the Laos Hmong in the refugee camps of Thailand were the Blue Hmong (literally "green" Hmong), or Mong Njua; the White Hmong, or Hmong Deaw; and the Striped Hmong. The Hmong dialects of all three groups differ, but are mutually understandable in most cases.

The dialects in China, however, differ from those in Laos and the United States.

Among the distinguishing characteristics of each group is the traditional clothing worn by women. Blue Hmong women traditionally wore elaborate indigo-dyed pleated skirts that were batiked and embroidered with silk materials. White Hmong women usually wore black pants and a long shirt with blue stripes; on ceremonial days they wore white pleated skirts. Striped Hmong are said to be a subgroup of the White Hmong. They wore striped armbands. Many of the Hmong in Laos and Thailand still dress this way regularly. In the United States, only the elders wear traditional dress regularly, although during Hmong New Year celebrations, even some of the young wear traditional dress. The New Year celebrations in Fresno, California, however, are now famous for their beauty pageants, in which Hmong women wear a great variety of clothing, including both American and traditional Hmong styles.

The Mien

Prior to the war, the Hmong and the Mien did not often encounter one another in Laos. Although linguists believe their languages are related (Matisoff, 1992), they are not mutually understandable in any way. While the Hmong almost always lived at the highest altitudes, the Mien preferred to farm a little lower down the mountains at three-thousand- to four-thousand-foot elevations, where there was a steady stream of water for agriculture and livestock.

Prior to the war, most of the Mien lived in northwest Laos along the Chinese border near Muong Sing, Nam Tha, and Phongsaly. As the war escalated and the Pathet Lao (Communist army) began encroaching, U.S. planes bombed northwestern Laos. In March 1967, the Mien and other mountain people were ordered to leave their villages. According to Crystal and Saepharn (1992, p. 363) the Mien were told that this was a "temporary evacuation," and "the advisors told the leaders that once the bombing campaign was completed, they could return to their highland valleys. The Mien abandoned their granaries that had been filled with the recent rice harvests, cash crops that had been stored in anticipation of itinerant Chinese merchants, and livestock, a rough indicator of families' accomplishments." The Mien recall that they were told to leave because the enemy was coming. Most walked for two to three months to the internal refugee camps established near Hwei Oh and Nam Keung.

As had been the case with the Hmong, by leaving the high mountains, where it is too cold for mosquitoes to carry malaria, many became exposed to malaria for the first time. Children and elders died during the trek, and all became dependent on rice drops from the United States that did not always arrive as scheduled.

Historians believe that although both the Hmong and the Mien came from China originally, the Mien came more recently. Some Mien refugees in the United States recall walking to Laos from China. They brought with them centuries of Chinese influence. Most notable is the influence of Taoism, which combined with their ancestral worship and animistic beliefs in spirits. As a result, the Mien are not only obligated to the spirits of their ancestors and the spirits of life, but to the "hundreds of deities in the Taoist pantheon, each of which plays a role in an individual's well-being" (Crystal and Saepharn, 1992). The Mien culture revolves around keeping families in line with this myriad of spirits. Pacifying these spirits is the responsibility of the male head of the household. Direct communication is conducted in ritual Chinese by male shamans.

Ritual Chinese was brought to Laos from China by a few Mien male scholars who were taught to read and write Chinese characters. A select few of the most talented Mien boys were also taught how to make and interpret Taoist paintings. The Mien built schools and hired teachers for these boys so they could also learn to write Taoist ritual texts and keep family genealogies and poetry in books made of bamboo paper (Crystal and Saepharn, 1992). These "passbooks" became the only recorded history of the Mien. It is now believed that as Mien have converted to Christianity, many have burned these recorded histories.

It was not until 1984 that a written, romanized script was adopted by the Mien. This occurred at a meeting in Portland, Oregon. The vast majority of Mien remain illiterate in their spoken language. Like the Hmong, the Mien culture is also based largely on an oral tradition.

In Laos, the Mien had about the same access to formal education as the Hmong. Because the Mien also lived in the mountains of Laos, school access and literacy for girls was almost nonexistent, as it was for the majority of boys. During the war, some Mien children attended the same rural schools built by the United States that the Hmong attended. However, according to Mien women now living in Richmond, California, some young Mien women from powerful families were sent to Vientiane to study nursing.

Although the Mien and the Hmong both have patrilineal traditions, the authority structure is not as strict in Mien communities. In addition, there are other marked distinctions between Mien and Hmong cultures that become more evident the longer these two communities live in the United States. The most notable distinction is that more Mien women know about and use contraceptives than Hmong women (Korenbrot, Minkler, and Brindis, 1988). As a result of delayed or lowered birthrates, more Mien women stay in school longer and work outside of the home as baby-sitters, factory workers, and house cleaners. More Mien women drive cars than Hmong women, a variable that greatly enhances their opportunities to earn outside income.

In the United States, the largest Mien communities are in northern California, in Richmond, San Pablo, Oakland, Sacramento, Redding, and Oroville. Smaller communities exist elsewhere in California, and in Oregon, Washington, and Alabama.

Other Minority Cultures of Laos

In addition to the Hmong and Mien, members of several other minority cultures from Laos came to the United States as part of the U.S. refugee resettlement commitment following the Vietnam War. In Laos, cultural minorities from the hills are collectively called

"Lao Theung," or "Lao of the hills." They include Khmu, Lua', Lahu, and Tai Dam. These communities are smaller than those of the ethnic Lao, the Hmong, and the Mien, and members often designate themselves as "Lao" rather than try to explain their ethnicity to Americans. Because there were so few members of these cultures, and because most adults had taken Lao names and were able to speak Lao, and because members of some cultures were as tall as ethnic Lao—in contrast to the Hmong, who typically are shorter—they have often been regarded as Lao in the United States. One of the unfortunate results is that some of the bilingual programs to which they have been assigned are Lao/English, even though the children speak neither language. Some programs have hired ethnic Lao assistants to help Khmu families, for example, even though Khmu mothers do not speak or understand Lao and many Lao look down on the Khmu and other minority cultures.

There are some basic similarities among all the Laotian minority cultures. Primary among them is the lack of an educational background in the family. According to Tayanin and Vang (1992, p. 7), "When families all worked together to grow crops and livestock in Laos, the children learned as they worked alongside the parents and other relatives. The father usually took responsibility for the boys and the mother took responsibility for the girls. Now mothers must look after their sons as well as their daughters, and fathers must be interested in guiding their daughters as well as their sons." Recent changes in the traditional gender division of labor has resulted in new parental responsibilities within all of these cultures.

Tayanin and Vang also point out that teachers must learn how to work with the entire extended family:

> Our children go to school and learn to speak English
> very quickly. Even so, they still have problems under-
> standing textbooks and writing essays. Khmu parents do
> not know what it is like to go to school, so it is easy for
> the children to fool the parents. The parents don't know

what the teachers expect them to do. Teachers tell them, "support your child in school." To the Khmu parents, support means to provide them with food and clothes and a place to sleep while they go to school. However, the teachers mean another kind of support: encourage your child, have books and magazines in the home, have regular mealtimes, bedtime, and study time, sit with your children while they study, take your children to visit the library and the zoo, and so on. [p. 59]

A book published by the Southeast Asia Community Resource Center in the Folsom Cordova Unified School District in California, entitled *Minority Cultures of Laos: Kammu, Lua', Lahu, Hmong and Iu-Mien* (Lewis, 1992), introduces most of these groups. The majority of these groups in the United States also live in California, although there are scattered populations in the Boston area and elsewhere.

The Lao

Approximately half of the total population of Laos is ethnic Lao. Culturally and linguistically, the Lao are dominant. Lao is the language of instruction in schools and the language of government, and more ethnic Lao than mountain people participate in government.

The Lao are related to the Thai. According to Jumsai (1971), "There is no difference between the Thai and the Lao" (p. 4). In the thirteenth century, both countries were ruled by King Rama Kamhaeng of Sukhotai, who in 1283 created the orthography (norms for writing and spelling) common to both countries (p. 5). Laos was colonized by the French at the beginning of the nineteenth century. French colonial ambitions for Thailand collided with the ambitions of the British (p. 8), resulting in a 1896 treaty that guaranteed the integrity of Thai territory. The American military based itself in Thailand throughout the Vietnam War and influenced the development of the Thai economy, but American military influence in Laos was limited to a supporting role because of a treaty of neutrality that the United States had signed with the Soviet Union at the beginning of the war. After the United States withdrew all military and economic support for Laos in 1975, Laos grew considerably poorer under the political domination of Vietnam and the Soviet Union. In contrast, Thailand still has a strong military aligned with the United States by recent history, and one of the fastest-growing economies in the world. Refugees from Laos who had fought for the U.S. military fled to Thailand.

Like the Thai, the ethnic Lao believe they are superior to the Hmong and other minorities, but many Thai also believe they are superior to the Lao. A study by Caplan, Whitmore, and Bui (1985) found that 62 percent of the ethnic Lao living in Orange County, California, and in Seattle, Boston, Chicago, and Houston had come from urban areas of their former country. Since there are so few urban areas in Laos, presumably this means that most of these Lao were from Vientiane. One indication that refugees tend to concentrate in areas where there are others from the same background is that, according to Rumbaut and Weeks (1986), 79 percent of the ethnic Lao living in San Diego were originally from rural areas.

Although the average Lao in the United States had almost five years of education when they arrived, there is a difference between the formerly rural Lao (who had little or no education) and the better-educated urban Lao (Caplan, Whitmore, Bui, and Trautman, 1985). As in many other parts of the world, education in Laos had been a class issue. According to Luangpraseut and others (1989), "having been to school was in itself a mark of socioeconomic standing in Lao society." There were few postsecondary schools in Laos. Elementary schools for the first three school years were built in rural areas of Laos beginning in the 1950s. As in urban areas, however, the government schools required children to wear uniforms and shoes and to purchase their own materials. Rice farmers often could not afford these expenses for all of their children and would send their children to school on alternate days sharing the same uniforms. Labor opportunity costs were a consideration in who was sent. So was gender. Usually boys were sent while girls stayed home to work. Poor rural families could not afford to relinquish all hands from the fields. After the first three years, children were sent to larger towns if parents could afford to pay for transportation, room, and board.

It is important to note that historically some ethnic Lao were opposed to secular education because it came from the French. Not only was a French model of discipline and structure imposed on the Lao, but to make matters worse, the French initially brought in Vietnamese teachers who spoke French to teach in Lao schools. All of the books were from France. Students were taught in a classical colonialist way about French history, French geography, and French literature, but nothing was taught about Laos. After the French were defeated at Dien Bien Phu and left Indochina in 1954, in accordance with the Geneva Accords the Americans began building rural schools and training teachers. In the early 1960s, the entire curriculum was changed to Lao language and Lao history.

As a less expensive alternative to state schools, Buddhist temples were a primary source of education for poor Lao boys. Girls, however, did not have access to education in the temples. The Lao practice Theravada Buddhism, which incorporates animistic beliefs in spirits and ancestor worship. At home, Lao children were traditionally taught a hierarchy of respect for, first, Buddha, then monks, then teachers, and then their parents. In Laos, children would make promises to their teachers at the beginning of each school year to be good, study hard, and not disappoint. At the end of the school year they brought presents to their teachers to beg forgiveness for not having lived up to their promises.

The Lao uphold a fairly strict gender division of labor. The story of Chitavanh Visathep explains the difference between being a Laotian teenage girl and being American:

Life is not the same as in Laos. Chitavanh is still learning American cultures and starting her new life. She tries to be more Americanized, but her parents still keep the old cultures and traditions. Both in American and Laos most Laotian children have a difficult time when they want to date. Children are allowed only to go to school and must come home as soon as possible, especially the girls. Most Laotian parents are extremely strict about their daughters. Some parents want their children to spend a lot of time studying and taking care of their younger brothers and sister. It's difficult for children because they want to go out and have good time with friends. They want to go out to see the light of the world. But children have to do as they are told. It doesn't matter how old you are as long as you still live at home. Chitavanh is the oldest of eight children and her parents felt it is her responsibility to help financially and personally with home duties. [Visathep, 1984, pp. 375–377]

The Vietnamese

The Vietnamese differ from the Hmong in most regards. They are traditional enemies. The Vietnamese were always a majority people, never a minority before coming to the United States. The Hmong and the Vietnamese have two important characteristics in common, however: a strong sense of identity and the importance of the family.

Historically, the Vietnamese shared a strong national identity that enabled them to oust the Chinese after a thousand years of occupation that ended in 938 A.D. The French, who began to colonize Vietnam in 1858, were finally defeated at Dien Bien Phu in 1954. American intervention in Vietnam began as the French phased out their operations, and ended in 1973. This strong national identity has in some cases been transported to American schools. The fierce independence as a people that has characterized Vietnam's history is to some extent a cultural norm of behavior.

Another similarity between the Vietnamese and the Hmong is that the extended family structure is very important in both cultures. According to Huynh Dinh Te (1988, p. 68), "Each member of the Vietnamese extended family has a special role to play, a responsibility to assume and a special authority to exercise vis-a-vis other members. This is reflected in a rather complicated kinship terminology."

Most Vietnamese refugees were from a higher socioeconomic background than other refugees from Southeast Asia. The majority, 83 percent, were from Saigon and other urban areas (Caplan, Whitmore, Bui, and Trautman, 1985). All but 1 percent were literate (Rumbaut and Weeks, 1986). Only 1.6 percent had no formal education. Thirteen percent had attended a university or other institution of higher education. Nearly one-quarter had graduated from high school.

Furthermore, Vietnamese women have the highest level of education of all the Southeast Asian refugee women; they also have the lowest fertility rate. Unlike Hmong women, Vietnamese women have played a frontline role in politics in their country. Perhaps the most significant events were the uprisings led by the Trung Sisters in 39 to 43 A.D. and by Lady Trung in 248 A.D. against the Chinese colonization that lasted from 111 B.C until 938 A.D.

Nevertheless, Vietnamese women perhaps were abused more during their escape than any other Southeast Asian refugee group. In 1981 alone the United Nations High Commissioner of Refugees (UNHCR) recorded 1,444 pirate attacks on boats carrying Vietnamese refugees in the South China Sea. As a result of these attacks, 961 people were killed or missing. Eight hundred fifty-seven women had been raped at least once by Thai pirates in the Gulf of Thailand (Refugee Reports, 1991). Some Vietnamese girls and women were taken on board the pirates' fishing vessels or to islands and gang raped repeatedly over extended periods of time. Reported attacks on boats declined to 534 in 1982, 162 in 1987, and 37 in 1990; but the violence continued. Although cooperation between the Thai and U.S. governments resulted in U.S. Coast Guard boats patrolling the Gulf of Thailand, 750 refugees were listed as dead or missing in 1989. Some camp workers believe that pirates dumped their victims' bodies overboard tied to heavy objects when they saw the large, white U.S. Coast Guard boats approaching.

The Vietnamese form of Buddhism is different from the Theravada Buddhism practiced by the Lao, the Cambodians, and the Thai. The Vietnamese blend Confucianism, Taoism, Animism, and Mahayana Buddhism (Huynh, 1988). A great number of the Vietnamese who came to the United States are Catholic, however, and many of their families have been Catholic since the sixteenth century.

Like the Hmong, Lao, and Mien languages, the Vietnamese language is tonal; and unlike Lao or Cambodian, the Vietnamese writing system is based on the Roman alphabet. From the sixteenth century until World War I, it was used primarily by Catholic priests. After World War I, the romanized alphabet began replacing the "chunom" characters that had been based on Chinese characters and used by common people. Today it is the only writing system used in Vietnam (Huynh, 1988).

The Chinese Vietnamese

A large number of Vietnamese refugees were ethnic Chinese who had been living in Vietnam for generations. Chinese Vietnamese identify themselves as such, and are regarded as a minority in Vietnam. Most of the Chinese Vietnamese refugees came from urban areas, where many had been merchants, according to the Rumbaut and Weeks (1986) study. According to their report, Chinese Vietnamese in San Diego had significantly lower average levels of education than ethnic Vietnamese, but this level was still higher than that of other Southeast Asian refugees. Eighteen percent of the Chinese Vietnamese were illiterate in any language. The Chinese Vietnamese women also have a higher fertility rate than ethnic Vietnamese women.

The Amer-Asians

Another group that has come to the United States from Vietnam are the children and families of American servicemen. "Amer-Asian" is a term that has been adopted for reference to these children. A 1985 study by the U.S. Catholic Conference found that the average American father had lived with the child's mother for two years in Vietnam (Felsman, Johnson, Felsman, and Leong, 1989). Abandoned or not, these children enter the United States under the highest and most protected priority for immigrants—immediate family reunification.

In general, these youngsters and their families were poor in Vietnam. They came from homes that had limited educational resources and low socioeconomic status (Chuong and Van, 1994). The U.S. Catholic Conference's 1985 study found that 13 percent of the mothers were housekeepers, one-quarter were street vendors, and almost one-third worked in nightclubs or restaurants (Felsman, Johnson, Felsman, and Leong, 1989). Many mothers sold things on the streets because after 1975 they could not get jobs with the new government because they had children with American fathers. These children performed significantly lower on educational measures in the United States than did other Vietnamese youngsters.

A 1988 study of children ages thirteen through seventeen born in Vietnam of American fathers found that they had the same average years of formal education as other Vietnamese teenagers—about three-quarters of both groups had up to seven years of formal education (Felsman, Johnson, Felsman, and Leong, 1989); but a larger proportion of those with American fathers, 13 percent, had no formal education at all, compared to only 2 percent of other Vietnamese teenagers. An even higher percentage, almost one-third, of teenagers with African American fathers had no formal schooling at all. All refugee teens are required to take an entrance test before beginning a special program called Preparation for American Secondary Schools (PASS). While 43 percent of all Vietnamese students scored above the beginning level of PASS, only 6 percent of those with American fathers did. About half of these youngsters said that "school and studying means very little to me," compared to a quarter of all Vietnamese students. The 1988 study raised questions about the quality of education received by youngsters in Vietnam who were part American (Felsman, Johnson, Felsman, and Leong, 1989), particularly those with African American fathers.

The Cambodians

The primary distinction among Cambodians, at least until 1975, was that of class between rural and urban people. Urban dwellers and wealthy Cambodians had more access to formal education than had rice farmers and those from fishing villages. However, regardless of their station in life, many Cambodians did not attend school on a regular basis between 1970 and 1975 because of the civil war and massive bombing of villages and towns. Families often lived in army camps when the father was in the army. There were no schools in most of these camps. Formal education ceased to exist for anyone between 1975 and 1980 during the government of Pol Pot and his Khmer Rouge.

Cambodians who fled their country in 1975 or earlier were spared the barbarism that ensued under Pol Pot. This group included members of the Lon Nol government, the royal family, and the economic elite who were immediately accepted for resettlement in the United States or France. Those with less clout remained at the Thai-Cambodia border for up to five years, waiting for refugee status to allow them to begin the process of resettlement elsewhere. The majority of Cambodians who were resettled in the United States, however, experienced or participated in the full horror of the Pol Pot regime.

This experience is well chronicled in a book by Molyda Szymusiak (1986). Szymusiak was a young girl during the Pol Pot regime.

She was later orphaned and adopted by Polish exiles living in France. Her autobiography, *The Stones Cry Out: A Cambodian Childhood, 1975–1980*, is a powerful testimony of how most Cambodian children lost their childhood. She described what she found while taking a break during a period at a girls' work camp:

> We climbed down from the trailer and went off, each looking for a little space to herself. A few meters away, under the trees, my aunt and I came upon several dead women: their stomachs were cut open, the entrails spilled out, and tufts of dry grass had been thrust into their orifices. I wanted to get away from them immediately, but other girls had come over to see. "Look at all those jewels!" The bodies were covered with necklaces, bracelets, rings. It was a great temptation to take one or two pieces of jewelry. . . . "Don't touch any of it," one of the girls said in a low voice. "The Yotears have put them there to see what we'll do." I think we might have met the same fate if we had let ourselves be tempted. [p. 68]

In a 1986 study of Indochinese psychiatric patients, Mollica, Lavelle, Wyshak, and Coelho found that their typical Cambodian patient had suffered an average of three times as many traumatic events in their lives as the average Lao, Hmong, or Vietnamese psychiatric patient. These traumatic events included lack of food or water, ill health, lack of shelter, imprisonment, war injury, torture, sexual abuse, social isolation, near death or witnessing death, being lost or kidnapped, witnessing murder or torture, and other events.

A watercolor painted by a Cambodian youth depicted a child witnessing the execution of his parents who were naked and tied back-to-back by the Khmer Rouge. Others showed emaciated human beings carrying baskets of skulls from piles of skulls under the orders of the Khmer Rouge. Still others showed children forced to watch as their fathers' innards were ripped out. Death was not always immediate. Boothby (1982, 1984) learned that many children witnessed their parents' slow starvation. Children older than age six were forced to leave their families and join work brigades, or they were sent into the interior in mobile units. When they arrived at the Thai border in 1979, most of the children had been abandoned and were severely malnourished. Boothby (1982) found that in the Khao-I-Dang refugee camp on the Thai-Cambodian border two years after the Vietnamese had invaded Cambodia and replaced the Pol Pot government, children were still haunted by recurring nightmares of past events they had witnessed, especially "children who had witnessed the death of a parent, particularly when violence had been involved." In 1985, the South Cove Community Health Center in Boston found that some Cambodian children still suffered from recurrent nightmares and bad memories of life under Pol Pot and the Vietnamese invaders (Lockwood, 1985).

Boothby (1982) was surprised to learn that in 1981 only a few of the Cambodian children in refugee camps in Thailand suffered from somatic problems, such as headaches, stiff necks, or temporary loss of eyesight or hearing that was unconnected to organic impairment. The unaccompanied minors in particular showed the tremendous resiliency of youth. Very few suffered from mental health disorders or exhibited behavior that Boothby regarded as overly aggressive, deviant, or manipulative. Boothby found that the child's age at the time of loss and a secured, on-going adult relationship after loss were the best predictors that unaccompanied children would adapt psychologically. According to Boothby (1982, p. 4), "Those who enjoyed solid, stable relationships with parents or others prior to the Khmer Rouge revolution seemed better able to withstand the loss of family and home. . . . Memories of a better time, along with internalized values learned from parents, culture and society were sources of comfort and courage." Boothby's research, however, was conducted in 1981, while the youngsters were still in the refugee camps. It remains to be seen what impact these experiences will have when these youngsters feel safe enough to allow their suppressed feelings to emerge. The occurrence of nightmares documented in 1981 and 1985 is evidence of such suppressed thoughts.

Cultures in Flux

I have tried here to distinguish Southeast Asian refugees from earlier immigrants from Asia and to provide a fair introduction to the Hmong, the Mien, the Lao, the Vietnamese, the Chinese Vietnamese, the Amer-Asians, and the Cambodians in terms of their cultures, languages, and religious beliefs. There are also major distinctions within each of these groups that shape the educational background of their children, such as how much formal education their parents have been exposed to, how strong their group identity is, and what they experienced during the war, during their escape, in the refugee camps, and since arriving in the United States. These differences are very important because without a general awareness of them, teachers can have no understanding of their students' home knowledge and cannot know how to begin to connect home and school learning. As mentioned in the introduction to this chapter, however, generalizations are only that, and those of us who accept them need to keep in mind that generalizations should never be applied directly to individuals, and that all cultures are in a constant state of change.

3

Educating Newcomers:
Lessons from Two Districts

So far, I have tried to show in a general way how the concept of Asian American academic success is predicated on a misleadingly simple understanding of Asian heritage. Simplified media impressions and misleading academic and statistical analyses have led to false stereotypes and a false sense that Asians are a monolithic group with few, if any, special needs in school.

I turn now from this general analysis to a closer look at the particular strengths and challenges presented by the Hmong. The case of the Hmong is enlightening because Hmong children represent an extreme example of the new challenges facing U.S. schools. Nevertheless, it is a case that is not unrepresentative of the general challenge presented by growing numbers of immigrant students from Asia and other parts of the world.

Since the mid 1960s, the majority of immigrants to the United States have not been of European origin, and according to the 1990 census, more immigrants entered the United States in the 1980s than in any other decade since the beginning of the twentieth century. The impact of the new immigrants on school districts has been great because they are younger at the time of their arrival, they tend to concentrate in certain areas of the country, and some groups have higher birthrates than native-born Americans. This is particularly true of the Hmong.

This chapter begins with two graphic examples of how school systems were caught unprepared by the great numbers of Southeast Asian refugee students that entered U.S. schools in the late 1970s and the 1980s. These examples present the experiences of two communities: one in Rancho Centro (a pseudonym for a city in the Central Valley of California), the other in Milltown (a pseudonym for a city in New England). The second part of the chapter explores the key similarities and differences in the responses of these two districts to this wave of immigration and migration, including the lack of preparation of teachers in both districts for dealing with Southeast Asian refugee students. The third part of the chapter elaborates on the need for better preparation of teachers, and reviews how school districts in general have made only limited efforts to deal with the needs of these students and their families by recruiting Hmong and other Southeast Asian teachers' aides or by providing career ladders for them to become credentialed bilingual teachers.

Getting Acquainted with the Challenge: Rancho Centro

At 7:00 A.M. on the first morning after Christmas vacation in January 1981, a principal arrived at her elementary school in Rancho Centro, California, to find a long line of people, many of them women wearing black embroidered turbans, waiting outside to register their children. Who were these people? Where had they come from? How did they find her school? Without knowing the answers to any of these questions, the principal, Jenny Dailey, opened the door, let them in, and headed for the telephone to call the superintendent's office. The people were from Laos, none of them spoke English, "and that was all we knew," Dailey recalled. "Four of us did nothing but register students from 7:15 until 5:30 that night," she remembered. When the assistant superintendent finally came out at about 10:30 in the morning, "he walked into my office and asked, 'What the hell is going on?'"

"In terms of preparation, we had none. We knew nothing about them," said Dailey. "We just stuck them right into classrooms. The teachers were most understanding. Lots of them had thirty-eight kids in their classes for a week or so." The school finally hired additional staff, but the new teachers were not trained to work with the Hmong, knew nothing of their culture, life experiences, family background, or language. Even so, the teachers were called "Hmong bilingual" teachers, because at that time California required a bilingual teacher when ten or more students spoke a language other than English.

In the following weeks, the Title I resource teacher and others set up classes to teach the new students beginning English vocabulary, how to follow instructions, and how to get around the building. The theme of these classes was, "What is this thing called school?" They went on walking tours. They practiced going through the line in the cafeteria. They practiced fire drills. Each new student was assigned a buddy, whose main job was to make sure the student used the bathroom. "Toilet training" was an activity that had to be taught. It did not arise in response to the children wetting their pants. "They did not know how to use the toilets and instead were squatting in the playground," Dailey said. What Dailey did not know was that in rural Southeast Asia there are few, if any, toilets, and that in the refugee camps where the children had lived before coming to the United States, it was perfectly acceptable for Hmong prepubescent children to squat outside.

Clothing was another problem. "Little girls were not wearing underpanties with their dresses," Dailey said. "Up until the third grade it was a constant battle, but that's with ourselves, of being unjudging and realizing that it wasn't anything naughty, but catching them and bringing them into the bathroom, explaining that whole rigamarole and pairing them up with older kids." Other children were wearing pajamas to school and being teased about it.

As things settled down, the children had to be taught that they were not supposed to come to school at 4:00 A.M., and that they had to go home after classes. "They liked school so much they wanted to stay there from sunup to sundown," Dailey said. Dailey and her team eventually created an after-school program to teach the students about American culture. It was taught by two Hmong men who knew a little bit of English. The school staff were amazed at the program's popularity. Dailey said:

> We intended it for the older kids for extra help; pretty soon forty to fifty kids would come for extra work. They would take all of the papers home so the parents could work on something. The whole family was learning. Kids would take all of the dittos from the trash for the family to study. The kids knew when the custodians after school would dump the waste baskets [and where] the teachers had dumped extra dittos. They would take like fifteen of the same one, for the mom, the dad, the sister, the brother. . . . They would take anything they could get their hands on to do at home.

Dailey and the other teachers soon learned that their greatest assets in learning about their new students were the refugees themselves:

> As far as information about the Hmong, Lao, Mien students we had, we pretty much did that on our own. We learned from them, mostly, from reading, from grabbing anybody who knew anything about it. The county school department came up with a book and had something about the culture of the Hmong, and mostly, though, when all was said and done, we ended up with three fathers who spoke a fair amount of English and some older students who had some English from living in other places in the United States. And we just talked to them and really got all of our information, the practical day-to-day information on students and/or parents.

Any publication on the new students or their culture or history was brought in and shared among teachers and administrators. The challenge brought about an increased cohesiveness among the teachers. "We are all there with a common need," said one teacher. In subsequent years, classes in Hmong culture were offered by the county school district. Many teachers took the classes to fulfill the requirement for a course on culture in order to become a certified language development specialist. "[Teachers] have to take Hmong culture, [but] they are also willing to because they are fascinated by it," the teacher said.

Karen Parish, whose program took students with special needs out of their regular classes for extra help in reading, became the school's "language resource teacher." Typical of the crisis response that dominated at the time was that she was given the title first and prepared for the job later. Parish had no previous training in teaching English as a Second Language (ESL), and she had no background in the cultures of her students. Although she began taking classes on teaching ESL through the Professional Development Center of the County Schools, these classes were not on language, but on techniques for teaching. "There was lots of training available, on techniques like 'total physical response,' and how to learn words as you use them," she said. She attended workshops in Rancho Centro and other school districts in the area.

Six years later, Parish and two half-time teachers established "language experiences" in the ESL curriculum at their school, such as lessons in learning to read through literature, vocabulary-development activities, and total physical response activities, such as jumping or sitting. By 1990, more than one-third of the 780 students in the school were Hmong.

The early response to Hmong students in this Rancho Centro school may have been faulty, but the most important thing for the refugees was knowing that the principal and teachers cared about them. Seven years later, however, the novelty of the Hmong had worn off. The school no longer did anything to help new Hmong students who came straight from the refugee camps in Thailand. Of those who arrived in 1987, Dailey explained, "Some kids adopted them. The ones in kindergarten and first grade had 'cousins' the teacher assigned them to on the first day," but "they were very frightened." The older kids self-selected their buddies. The other Hmong children were "very compassionate, very helpful." While this may suggest that the schooling of refugee children was under more control than when the Hmong first arrived, it may also suggest that an attitude of benign neglect was setting in.

A Second Example: Milltown

What happened in Rancho Centro is typical of other places around the country that received large numbers of Southeast Asian students. Another example is Milltown, located on the East Coast. Milltown is where I first heard a Hmong say publicly that Southeast Asian children, including Hmong, were not receiving an equal education, and that schools were not making adequate efforts to help Hmong become certified teachers.

As in Rancho Centro, teachers and administrators in Milltown had no idea who their new students were when they began arriving in the late 1970s. An elementary school teacher described what happened:

> In '78 and '79, the Hmong were coming into the west section. I was teaching at [Hillcrest] that year. That year the school was unprepared. I started out with a complete Anglo class; by the end of the year 50 percent of my class was Hmong. The only reason I know they all were Hmong—I had no idea which was which—I came to [my elementary school] and I found one Laotian boy. I said to him, "How come you're here?" [He said,] "We have moved out of that neighborhood because we're Laotians and they're all Hmong."

Initially, the schools hired "Hmong bilingual" teachers to help with the influx, but they were neither Hmong nor bilingual. Teachers soon realized that their best source of information was the refugees themselves.

Jessica Barrimore, a Milltown elementary principal, likened her own lack of preparation to her experience in the 1960s, when she became the principal of a predominantly African American elementary school. She explained: "I had no courses or training to prepare me, a white person, to be a principal in a practically all black school. The people that helped me [were] not [in] the school department; it was the teachers' aides who worked along with me. It was the community that opened their doors and let me into their homes. That's how I got my training in the black community, really."

An African American teacher responded to Barrimore's comments:

> That's just what they're used to, the parents of the students, to be aides in the classroom, regardless of their education. A lot of the tension could be relieved because these parents could go back into the community [and say] 'They're doing this and this, this is what you should do with your child.' It will help those people know that they are valued and they're just as much a part of our community as everybody else. The kids see [role models] and they say, hey, we could be this, we could be that.

Barrimore suggested that there was a conflict between what principals were expected to do and what they were prepared to do:

> [I] never had a principal's workshop in that. You received federal guidelines and then the program, but it was all organization and management. It's a policy of the school department that the principal is a business manager. I fight that role, constantly. You are to become a manager,

a paper pusher. That's not why I went into education, that's not why I became a principal. You have to fight the administration to get curriculum specialty work, public relations, human relations, because they will knock you down with papers and forms. Workshops are on preparing the budget, managing the custodian.

Principals were expected to monitor the children's reading progress, for example, but Principal Barrimore did not have the preparation to do that. She explained, "Principals had no preparation whatsoever for dealing with the population they deal with. We weren't prepared at all. I had no preparation. None. There wasn't any. They arrive and you kind of get the idea of working along with them. You get to know them, as children really. It becomes more of a melting pot. You assimilate them into the school."

Barrimore thought that principals would benefit from in-service training on the cultures and backgrounds of their students. She said, "Definitely, we could use additional support and information. I know I could, and I think most other principals could definitely. The more you know to work with them. . . ."

Barrimore explained that "teachers received more training" than principals—"after the fact, though. I don't think Milltown was ready for this when [the refugees] first arrived." At the district level, however, Milltown administrators seemed to feel that teachers were prepared enough for Southeast Asian students. One said, "We feel we have addressed those problems." The person in charge of in-service training for bilingual teachers at the district's Office of Bilingual Education said, "We moved away from cultural awareness. We're doing a lot more with implementation of curriculum, curriculum development. We've been in the business long enough that I believe we're past the superficial kinds of things in terms of who are these people, what is their culture, what are their languages like, contrastive analysis of languages, we've done that in the past."

There is still a need for curriculum development in Milltown schools. One of the Southeast Asian resource teachers who works in the classroom with teachers said, "I don't know if they have a curriculum or not." There is also a continuing need for cultural awareness. In contrast to what administrators said about adequate preparation, an elementary teacher said, "We get a little, not much at all." Barrimore said in-service training was provided "just in the very beginning for people who are new teachers to ESL or bilingual classes." Barrimore said, "[There was] very skimpy information. In the beginning we did have a very good fellow who did cultural background. Everyone had to take those courses. The courses weren't as informative as the actual in-services that they gave in the beginning when the Hmong first came. We had Hmong language training."

Ironically, even though new refugees were still arriving directly from the camps in Thailand in the late 1980s and early 1990s, the preparation of new teachers, counselors, and administrators had deteriorated.

Differences and Similarities

These introductions and the following sections illustrate four clear differences in how schools on opposite ends of the country responded to Hmong, Cambodian, and Lao students. First, the Hmong arrived suddenly, en mass, in Rancho Centro, while in Milltown they arrived over time and in fewer numbers. Milltown teachers, however, were confronted with Cambodian, Hmong, Lao, and some Vietnamese students all at the same time, making it more difficult for them to learn about or identify the particular cultural traits of any single group. Second, the community in Rancho Centro heartily welcomed the Hmong, while the Milltown community hoped that all Southeast Asian refugees, including the Hmong, would go away. Third, teachers asked for help in Rancho Centro in meeting the special needs of the new students. In Milltown, administrators thought that teachers had enough background on the different cultures and languages to make do on their own. Finally, one man in Rancho Centro managed to broker a two-way interaction between the schools and the Hmong community; in Milltown, after ten years the schools had only one Cambodian resource teacher and a Hmong home liaison, neither of whom were initially regarded as resources for teachers, principals, and counselors to learn about Southeast Asian students. Table 3.1 summarizes the differences in how Rancho Centro and Milltown responded to Hmong students.

The Settings

The settings themselves, Milltown and Rancho Centro, are a study in contrast.

Milltown

Milltown is an old city that has long been an important port and industrial center. While there is a tradition of New England gentility in Milltown, immigrants have long been a defining characteristic of the city. Since the early nineteenth century, immigrants have worked its factories, inhabited its residential neighborhoods, and attended its public schools. In the nineteenth and early twentieth centuries, large numbers of Irish, Italians, African Americans, and Jews settled in this city. Later, the Portuguese came, many from the Azores. But since the mid 1970s, the demographics of Milltown, now a city of 155,000 people, have changed dramatically. Most recently, large numbers of Spanish-speaking immigrants and refugees from Central America, Puerto Rico, the Dominican Republic, and Columbia have made their homes in the area, some by way of New York. In the midst of this demographic shift, the arrival of more than fourteen thousand Southeast Asian refugees, including three thousand Hmong, was not considered special.

Southeast Asian refugees originally were resettled in Milltown because three local nonprofit organizations sponsored them through contracts with the U.S. Department of State. The organizations agreed to provide for the refugees during their first month of arrival.

Because the state has so many refugees for its size, the law specified that the only new arrivals allowed directly from camps would be immediate relatives. Secondary migration, however, has increased the total number of Southeast Asians in this city.

Most Hmong and Cambodians in Milltown live in the poorest housing on the southern side of town. They often live in old duplexes and walk-ups that have been further subdivided into small apartments. Many of these buildings need repairs, but they are owned by slumlords who do little to maintain them. I visited two Hmong homes in Milltown. The contrast showed how different the resettlement experience can be. One was a well-kept, large Victorian house with a wide front porch, a fenced-in yard, and an old maple tree on the sidewalk. In the middle of the living room was a small, portable black-and-white television that appeared to stay turned on permanently, regardless of whether anyone was watching it. The house appeared to have come furnished, with a couch and overstuffed chairs, a dining table, and a china cabinet—not the kinds of purchases Hmong would ordinarily make. Three or four families lived in the house, and all of them were related. The house was very jovial and filled with children. It reminded me of the cheerful atmosphere of the Ban Vinai refugee camp, but in a Norman Rockwell setting.

I also visited a Hmong family with two children who had just arrived from Thailand. They lived in a one-bedroom apartment on the third floor of a dark brown triple-decker typical of the buildings in which most refugee families live in Milltown. The building was squeezed between other buildings on a street of triple-deckers exactly like it. There was no yard. In the apartment, there was no furniture except three folding chairs that had been borrowed for our visit. The wooden floor has been scrubbed so hard that it shined. My general impression during that brief visit was that there was very little happiness and a lot of stress in that house. While the mother talked to me, her small son screamed in a bedroom. The father emerged briefly, looking very angry. We heard hits and then muffled

Table 3.1 How the Milltown and Rancho Centro Schools Responded to Changing Demographics.

	Positive	Negative
Activities in/ Aspects of Milltown Schools	Two Cambodian resource teachers work in the schools.	There is no designated Hmong cultural broker.
	Three paraprofessional counselors work in the schools.	Paraprofessionals are not respected as resources.
	The state department of education is aware of problems in ESL.	Administrators think teachers have had enough cultural training.
		Southeast Asians have no clout in teachers' union.
Activities in/ Aspects of Rancho Centro Schools	A Hmong classroom teacher was hired in the 1990s.	No Hmong counselors work in the schools.
	The schools welcomed newcomers.	No paraprofessional counselors work in the schools.
	Special meetings introduced parents to the schools.	Title VII activities only benefit certain ESL teachers.
	The county offered a Hmong culture course to teachers.	Hmong parents are no longer introduced to schools.
	There was a Hmong cultural broker in the Title VII program.	CBEST is a barrier for aspiring Hmong teachers.
	Title VII provides in-service training for Hmong aides.	
	Title VII provides a career ladder for Hmong aides.	
	In-service training for teachers is ongoing.	
	Schools developed materials and curriculum for newcomers.	

Activities/Aspects Common to Both Schools	
Caring individuals reached out to refugee communities.	The schools were not prepared for changing student demographics.
Southeast Asians are working in the schools.	Site administrators were least prepared for new students.
Teachers are receiving some in-service training.	Teachers were not prepared by universities or colleges.
Teachers are aware that they need more training.	School districts did not support career ladders for Hmong.
Teachers like the Hmong and other Southeast Asian students.	Students need Southeast Asian counselors at all levels.
	Southeast Asians working in the schools are underpaid.
	Schools do not know how to work with refugees as resources.
	Cultural in-service training is not adequate for teachers.
	Most Hmong students are tracked low and are not college bound.
	Hmong students are segregated from mainstream students.
	Hmong parents believe that children receive an unequal education.
	Students in ESL programs may be missing subjects.
	Communicative ESL strategies do not offer grammar.

cries. Outside, a typhoon raged, bringing a tree crashing through the back of the house. We found the street covered in tree branches when we emerged. Yet the mother sat silently until I suggested ending our meeting early. I cannot speculate what was going on in this mother's mind, but I knew that she was very tense, and her stoic behavior suggested that this was not the first time she had been unable to change her environment.

Rancho Centro

In contrast to the industrial core of Milltown, Rancho Centro is a city of sixty thousand people in an agricultural region. In 1988, California joined New Mexico as the first states in the country with a majority of minority students in their public schools. In California in 1993 to 1994, more than one in six children in the public schools were born in another country; more than one in four spoke a language other than English at home; more than one out of every five students were classified as LEP (California Department of Education, 1994). Approximately 77 percent of the children in this category were Spanish speakers. The rest spoke Vietnamese, Chinese, Hmong, Cambodian, Lao, Mien, and more than fifty other languages.

The state of California has experienced a vast increase in the number of Southeast Asians in its schools in recent years. It originally received more refugees directly from the Southeast Asian refugee camps than any other state. Family reunification and secondary migration have further increased that number. About 40 percent of all the Southeast Asians in the United States, an estimated six hundred thousand people, now live in California (LaVally, 1993). Most of the Southeast Asian refugees in California live in the San Francisco Bay Area, the Central Valley, the Los Angeles basin, and the San Diego metropolitan area. The Southeast Asian population in these areas is continuing to increase rapidly due to high fertility rates and family reunification immigration. Demographic trends indicate that California's schools have only begun to deal with the challenge presented by this group.

More than in any other area of the country, California's Central Valley has experienced a large and sudden influx of Hmong. Rancho Centro has one of the highest percentages of Hmong of any community in the country. Estimates of the Hmong population range from eighty-five hundred to ten thousand, roughly one-sixth of the total population. More than one-third of the elementary school student population was Southeast Asian in 1990. The Hmong arrived in this community largely as a result of secondary migration. They had originally been resettled in places like Seattle, Philadelphia, Portland, and San Diego; but for a number of reasons, including low-cost housing and warm weather, they later chose to move to the Central Valley's major cities, including Rancho Centro.

One reason the Hmong came to the United States was in hopes of finding a "future," by which they mean land to farm, safety, and a community of other Hmong. Word spread among Hmong communities in other parts of the United States that a Hmong man had become a successful farmer in Fresno, also in the Central Valley (Bliatout, Downing, Lewis, Yang, 1988). Some families then sent scouts ahead. The cities of the Central Valley were caught unprepared when in 1981 Hmong began arriving in great numbers, seemingly overnight.

Rancho Centro is a relatively prosperous city, with an economy based on agriculture. The appearance of Rancho Centro is that of a young and growing city. There is also a large Spanish-speaking community, and there are many farmworkers' children in its schools. Most families live in single-level dwellings or apartments with yards. Many of them are made of stucco, painted light shades of white, yellow, and other pastel colors.

Differences

The biggest difference between the responses of the two communities was that Rancho Centro welcomed the newcomers. In fact, the assistant superintendent in the Rancho Centro High School District was worried that the Hmong would move on and the district would lose its state and federal funding for bilingual students.

The assistant superintendent for elementary schools said, "It's inexplicable how well . . . they were received in the community." Over and over again I was told heartwarming stories by teachers and administrators about other teachers and administrators, and community people, who did "everything they could think of to help these people, make it easier for them." At one school, a teacher told her mother that the Hmong children did not have any toys. The mother told a group of her friends who then collected old dolls and made new outfits so that every one of the Hmong girls in the elementary school received a doll for Christmas. The boys were given marbles. Rancho Centro civic leaders met regularly to think of positive steps to help integrate the newcomers.

The Milltown school district did not welcome Southeast Asian youngsters. A high school teacher told me he suspected that the school district was ignoring the "refugee problem" in hopes that it would go away, that the refugees would move on to California or somewhere else. The Hmong trickled into Milltown over a ten-year period along with Laotians, Cambodians, and Vietnamese, and they arrived just before an even larger influx of Spanish-speaking immigrants. Milltown has not welcomed the Hmong any more than it has welcomed the Spanish-speaking newcomers. With the exception of the efforts of a local foundation, a Catholic nun, a political activist, and a few other individuals and organizations, little has been done to integrate the newcomers into the community at large.

The contrast in how the Hmong were received in California and New England in part reflects differences in tradition between the East and West Coasts. In Milltown, ethnic differences are firmly entrenched, and class distinctions are closely guarded. In California, however, in the early 1980s, a time of relative prosperity, Californians prided themselves on living in a land of opportunity, and they were more open, on the surface at least, to offering a helping hand to the Hmong. That attitude changed dramatically in the 1990s, a period of continued economic recession that resulted in the growing resentment of newcomers who relied on public assistance (Walker-Moffat, 1994). Ethnic and class barriers do exist in California, but they are more subtle than in the East. Asian Americans, however, are a well-established minority in California; the first Chinese came in the nineteenth century, and most of the state's major cities had large populations of Japanese, Filipinos, Chinese, and other Asian groups before the arrival of the Southeast Asians.

Because of these differences in character, I expected to find that Rancho Centro schools were able to respond better to the challenges posed by the Hmong. Among other things, I expected to find that teachers could concentrate on Hmong culture since there were few Southeast Asians in this community who were not Hmong. Milltown teachers had to learn about and respond to the backgrounds and learning styles of several other Southeast Asian ethnic groups. In hindsight, it probably would have made no difference if all of the Southeast Asians in Milltown were Hmong; they still would not have been treated with special attention. Likewise, Rancho Centro would have probably welcomed any other Southeast Asian group as they welcomed the Hmong.

Not only did Rancho Centro welcome the newcomers, but the teachers recognized that they themselves needed help, and they asked for it. As one Rancho Centro administrator said, "We're just beginning to learn what questions to ask." Rancho Centro teachers were anxious to know more about their new students, their culture, their background, their families. Most of all, they wanted to know what to teach the Hmong and how to teach it. In Rancho Centro the school district provided ongoing in-service workshops for its teachers, and the county provided courses in Hmong language and Hmong culture and in teaching methodologies, including ESL and Sheltered English. In-service workshops on cultural, language, and background issues were provided to Milltown teachers only in the early years after the Southeast Asians first arrived. Yet the fact remains that site administrators, teachers, and counselors in both Rancho Centro and Milltown did not receive adequate preparation or in-service workshops.

A high-level administrator working in the Milltown Office of Bilingual Education told me that, "All courses are given bilingually or by bilingually trained teachers." In fact, there were no Hmong, Lao, Vietnamese, or Cambodian classroom teachers and no teachers who spoke these languages in the Milltown schools. The administrator said that most of the bilingual classes were actually ESL classes. He pointed out that "there are not large numbers of professionals [from these communities] who can work in their own language." He said that if he had three wishes and the funding to implement them, he would hire professional consultants to address issues related to the Southeast Asian population. He would also increase the teaching staff, but he recognizes that this would burden the community, in terms of cost and the necessity to reallocate resources or raise taxes. Third, he would immerse those students who do not speak English in regular classrooms rather than put them in so-called bilingual classrooms that are not really bilingual.

Without the ability to converse with students in their first languages, teachers in Milltown said they needed more materials and aides in order to be better teachers. An elementary school teacher suggested, "My thought is there should be an aide in every classroom in inner-city schools because the children need so much attention." An elementary principal said that she would "do away with remedial programs (math and reading), and put the emphasis on aides in the classroom, if you had to make that choice." A teacher in Milltown said, "the problem is we're so limited in translators. We have a Laotian. If we have a problem with a Cambodian or a Hmong child, we have to call the administration office and they have to send someone up. Sometimes it could take days."

Both Milltown and Rancho Centro teachers regarded Hmong aides primarily as translators. Neither set of teachers fully grasped the fact that there is no substitute for a solid background in the cultures of the students they teach. The Cambodian resource teacher in Milltown said the teachers "profit nothing" from mere translation. Another common problem was lack of in-service training for aides.

Aides in Milltown received no in-service training, while in Rancho Centro, only those aides working in the Title VII program benefited from monthly in-service workshops. In neither district did in-service workshops provide a forum for aides to offer their own insights.

Despite the recognition by teachers and counselors that they needed help meeting the unusual challenges of Southeast Asian students, the schools did not making effective use of Southeast Asians already working in the schools, or tap the tremendous resources that existed in the refugee communities in their areas. Teachers needed the language and cultural skills that Southeast Asians could provide, but they did not work with the Southeast Asians as partners. The teachers did not turn to aides for advice or input in a two-way cultural exchange. Teachers regarded Southeast Asian aides, home liaisons, and resource teachers as interpreters.

Similarities

The response of these two school districts to the influx of large numbers of Hmong students shared three general characteristics. First, caring individuals in both districts, some of whom were in fact teachers and administrators, took the lead in learning about the new students. Second, teachers, administrators, and counselors generally were not taught how to facilitate two-way communication between the schools and the refugee communities by using parents, aides, and home liaisons as resources and cultural brokers, to see them as more than just interpreters. Third, the districts were inhibited by the lack of adequate funding.

Caring Individuals

In the vacuum created by the lack of a national policy addressing newcomer students' needs, the slack has had to be taken up in community after community by caring individuals. These are people who have made it their personal responsibility (beyond their official duties or job description, and often on their own time) to go into refugee homes to learn about Southeast Asian immigrants.

The Rancho Centro elementary school principal was one such person. When the influx began, she said, "There was so much going on that year. At ten o'clock at night I wouldn't know where I was or why I was there. All this while I was running around like a hen with its head cut off, trying to attack it from as many different fronts, trying to get the parents in touch with the people they needed to get in touch with. The teachers in the classrooms were remaining real calm and real smooth and just doing a bang-up job in terms of teaching English."

Often, the caring person was a first- or second-generation immigrant or a member of another minority group who could relate to the refugee experience. The fact that African American, Latino, and other recent immigrants could relate to the experiences of the children of people who had come from the top of mountains in Laos sheds some light on the challenge of being African American or Latino in American schools. José Rafael, a guidance counselor at Rancho Centro High School and the director of its Newcomer Program, explained that he did not need special preparation to work with Southeast Asian youngsters because he had begun school speaking only Spanish. He knew what it was like to speak a language other than English and to come from a culture other than Anglo.

As an African American principal working in a predominantly European American field, Sally Fulton of Milltown provided the following insights about Southeast Asians: "They are perceived to be less than they are because they look so different, and I don't mean physically, I mean their habits. This group, because they are welfare recipients, it has been a stigma on them. Because there are a large number of children, that stigmatizes them. They don't dress the way we think Western people should dress. It's really going to be rough for them to overcome this. I know, I had to."

Other caring individuals had similar experiences. The director of bilingual, bicultural education programs in Rancho Centro also drew on her African American identity. She knew the Southeast Asians would have to fight for everything they deserved. In Seattle, another teacher I met said she could relate to the newcomers because she was the daughter of a Norwegian immigrant; and one of the most active ESL teachers in Seattle, an immigrant from Hong Kong, said she lived in the International District, where students often knocked on her door in the same way they would have done in Asia. The former director of the bilingual program in a major U.S. city who had immigrated from Nanking, China, and begun his work life in the United States as an assistant custodian eventually became a classroom aide, and then a teacher, and was very active in promoting the career development of aides so that they could become teachers.

Dom DePetri, a guidance counselor in Milltown and a former ESL teacher, said he knew that when immigrant students entered the doors to their own homes, they entered a different world. According to DePetri, "Immigrant kids today have an unbelievable burden, because their parents are coming from an antiquated society into a supermodern world. I feel bad for the parents, and I always tell the kids you have to understand [that] your parents grew up one way, and they expect you to grow up the same way. And the kids do understand this. I came from an immigrant family, and I know you walk into the house and, zip, you have to make the adjustment."

Two-Way Communication

The key element missing in both school districts was a system established to ensure that two-way communication occurred between the schools and the refugee communities. Teachers, principals and counselors need to be taught how to work with parents, aides, and home liaisons as resources and cultural brokers, rather than merely using them as interpreters. These parents want to participate in their children's education, but they need outreach programs that connect home and school learning. A wealth of interest and commitment has not been tapped. As a result, teachers and administrators have failed to reach parents, community leaders, and many of the students themselves.

Parent Participation

In Milltown, the director of a Southeast Asian organization and the father of ten school-age children pessimistically assessed that the power of the teachers' union was so great that it prevented the system of parental oversight from operating. He asked, "So what [are] the teachers doing? Are they just following their own liberation? [Don't teachers have any guidelines?] They have help from the parent-teachers organization. [The PTO] can follow what the teachers are doing in the schools for the kids. But all of the structures are run by the union, so no more function."

Non-Asian community leaders, like Sister Julian, a Catholic nun who ran a school for refugees in Milltown, claim that school districts use parents. They put together groups that include Southeast Asian parents, but never ask their advice, only tell them what to do. Sister Julian said that it is common practice for schools and charity groups to "put token Southeast Asians on a board, and they never ask them a question. They talk around them. It happens over and over again. But the board looks like an ideal setup." Sister Julian gave the example of "a PTA for minority parents; they never ask the parents what their problems are. They are not listening. Or they set it up and call them in and say, 'This is how it is going to work.' It's nice to have report cards translated into Cambodian and Hmong, but the poor parents can't even read Cambodian and Hmong. Have you ever had a simple meeting where you told them what social studies is? What is the value of a child taking that subject?"

Sister Julian said that a Southeast Asian community organizing group met several times to voice complaints to the superintendent and assistant superintendent about the busing program that caused their children to be sent to different schools around the city to fill minority slots, and about the lack of Southeast Asian aides in the schools. The new superintendent set up an Indochinese Advisory Council of ten people. They met a few times, but "we have a long way to go," she said. Sister Julian said that the problem is the teachers' union and the seniority system. "Beginning in the cafeteria, they are protecting their jobs" from the Southeast Asians; "it gives you a headache."

Joua Kue, a Hmong who worked in the bilingual office of the Milltown school district for twelve years, said,

> Milltown used to have a meeting of a group of Southeast Asian parents meeting about continuing problems, what they should do in the schools, what the teachers should do to meet the needs of the children. But that program I can see is not for input of the community to the school, but only to perform whatever the school asks [refugee parents] to do. So they can only do certain things. [The parents] don't have a chance to fix or direct the goals of the school. They just sit there and listen and sign whatever paper they have to sign to get more grants.

The potential for real dialogue between the schools and Southeast Asian community groups and parents could not be greater. After years of regimented life in refugee camps, school is often the only scheduled event for Southeast Asians in the United States. They want to learn what school is all about and participate in the education of their children. Unlike American-born parents, Hmong parents want to use the education their children receive to help themselves deal better with American culture and society. As Geddes (1976, p. 72) found in Thailand, "The younger generations are the pioneers," and "the new relationships they make become the focal points" of their parents' security in changing circumstances.

Parents need translators in order to participate in their children's schools. They have shown their willingness to learn by attending meetings. Parents eagerly attended initial parent meetings at Principal Dailey's school in Rancho Centro. Dailey explained that initially they had lots of parent meetings, began maybe a week, two weeks after the Hmong arrived, simply to explain our school system, the importance of proper dress—big problem with time: they were here at the crack of dawn and they did not want to go home—to let parents know what we were doing with their children and when their children came home, the kinds of things we would like them to reinforce and to answer any questions. . . . We anticipated about fifty to sixty people, but all of the parents and the whole extended family came. There were approximately 120 in the library; you couldn't breathe. We had brought cookies and punch. The more we brought, the more they ate. We refilled the cookie tray four times, they were stuffing their pockets. The meetings usually last forty-five minutes; this lasted three and a half hours and it only broke up because I had another meeting.

Communication gaps still exist. Dailey described how at one parent conference there were two fathers, a Hmong gentleman and a Lao gentleman, who interpreted for the others. "We would say something, the Lao man would speak to the Lao half of the room. Then the Hmong man would stand up and speak to the Hmong. The Hmong would ask him a question and he would ask us a question. It would always bother me a little bit because I would say something I thought was very profound, and he would say it over here and people would laugh." Dailey seems to have misunderstood the laughter of the Hmong and the Lao parents. They may have laughed because they were embarrassed by what she said, or because the information was new, or because they wanted her to know that they felt good about what she said, or that what she said did not translate easily, and the interpreter was explaining that he did not fully understand her. The parents were extremely grateful; Dailey said: "The response from those parents—one parent who moved

[away] and came in [beforehand] and in very broken English gave us so many compliments, [about] how much we cared, how much we worked, how many extra things we had done for the children. It's a wonderful experience for us."

There is an ongoing need for special meetings for parents who have had little or no education themselves, and for interpreters in meetings for all parents. Nevertheless, since the first year of Hmong migration to the Central Valley, very little has gone on in parent education. Principal Dailey's school no longer has special parent meetings for the Hmong. Dailey explained: "We had two more basic information meetings, and then we had our first parent conference, a group conference, a teacher in the library with this whole sea of Hmong parents. We didn't have enough interpreters. If they had any specific questions, they'd ask the teacher."

An example of how different interpretations of events can occur was an August 1987 meeting for all parents of incoming kindergarten students. Approximately 40 percent of the 375 parents who showed up were Hmong. The assistant superintendent was very pleased with the turnout. He said that Micah Vang, a Hmong scholar who worked in the Rancho Centro schools for years, did some translating. Vang, however, said that the reason why so many Hmong showed up at the meeting was because he had encouraged them to go by telling them that they must do this for their children; yet when they got there they found that the district had not provided any translators, and the Hmong parents did not understand what was going on. Vang went to the meeting because he was interested, not because he was paid and assigned to go. He did his best to translate a little, but most of the Hmong parents left. Vang said, "I know for sure why parents don't want to come to meetings. Very large gap in translations to them, so they don't understand. Went to several meetings. All the Hmong parents left because no one said it in Hmong, and they don't know what to do or how to do it. Still goes on."

Vang said that the Hmong who have been in the United States

the longest, the first wave who came before 1983, came to all the meetings that they were invited to, but that the most recent arrivals are still in transition: "They are still arranging their life." Vang said:

> It depends on the excitement; if they know they come for nothing, they won't come. . . . You really have to excite them, call them, push them a little bit. When I sent out five hundred papers to those parents, about fifty came to our meetings. Thirty of them came before '83. The others, if I really want them to come, I have to address personal letters to them. Sometimes I send three or four languages. Last year, I sent letters and then I call them one or two days before the meeting. I have my colleagues [Hmong] call them. It seems to be the most efficient way to [recruit them].

Hmong parents do not fully understand why their children go to school. They know it is to learn English, to help them become like Americans, and to earn a diploma. They do not know why else. Vang asked parents at a meeting, if their children start school early, will they have more success? They said, "Yeah, if they go to school very early they will have more chance to learn more English, and they will be more successful in school." Vang said, "'So you think going to school and learning more English will make your children more successful.' They said 'yeah.' I said, 'What about Anglo student? They speak English perfectly already so they don't need to go to school.'"

Ironically, a high school teacher in Milltown said, "We felt we have been very successful" because parents came to meetings to pick up their children's report cards. The assistant superintendent of the elementary district said that there is a line of communication in the Hmong community. A complaint usually goes out to an "ambassador," who usually goes to the teacher.

Rancho Centro elementary principal Fulton found that the parents were trying to learn from their children: "Even I find that the parents will help the child a little with the homework, but I think it's not so much that they're helping, but that they're trying to figure what's going on and learn along with them." Education often involves the entire family. A parent said, "I teach him, he teaches me." Fulton suspected that the children were embarrassed about their parents. She said, "Although no child has ever said it to me, I sense the child's displeasure at the apparent inability to cope with this system. They don't say 'I don't like my mother and father,' but they're not pleased that their parents can't come like the American parents."

The Role of the Cultural Broker

Rancho Centro was very fortunate to have a single individual who was able to take on the role of cultural broker. Micah Vang gave everything he could to the school district. He was able to act freely because one administrator realized they needed Vang and was willing to fight for him to make sure that he could do whatever he felt needed to be done. The reason the administrator was willing to fight for Vang was that she herself was from an ethnic minority, so she recognized the need for a Hmong person on her staff. The reason he was accepted by others, however, was because he had been educated in France and was considered by teachers to be different than uneducated Hmong.

Joua Kue of the Milltown office of bilingual education could have fulfilled the same role as Vang did, but he had been frustrated in his attempts to inform teachers and Hmong students because he lacked formal credentials and did not hold a "professional" position. No one had recognized that he was a valuable asset, or that he could have been doing a lot more to advise teachers, counselors, and parents about Hmong students. The reason most often cited for this oversight was, as has already been mentioned, that members of the teachers' union perceived bilingual personnel as a threat to their own jobs. While the president of the teachers' union recognized the need for Southeast Asian aides and for more teacher training on Southeast Asian culture, she said that union support for hiring bilingual personnel was contingent on a growing population that would safeguard the existing jobs for teachers and counselors.

Vang's value in Rancho Centro was that he could do all that the regular resource teachers in Milltown were doing, and he could do it better because he was part of the culture he served, he understood the accepted norms of behavior in Hmong culture, and he spoke Hmong. In his role, he tested new students for placement, and he visited the various schools and worked with individual students when necessary. His role may have been even more important than that of the resource teachers because he acted and functioned as a cultural broker between the schools and the Southeast Asian community. Vang handled problems involving transportation, and he taught courses to teachers, who received graduate-school credits for passing. Yet, the Cambodian resource teachers in Milltown received a teacher's salary, and Vang did not.

People like Vang can be found at local community colleges, where they are often struggling to earn credentials so they can apply for positions in the public schools; but in order to hold onto such people once they have been employed, schools must give them respected positions with recognized responsibilities, and pay them accordingly. Vang did not receive these things. He has since left the school district.

The Federal Role in Providing Education for Refugees

Having discussed some key similarities and differences between the responses of Milltown and Rancho Centro and those of the Hmong and other new Asian groups, it is important to step back for a moment and examine why it is that these school districts were presented with these problems in the first place. Primarily, it was the direct result of U.S. intervention in the Southeast Asian conflicts of the 1960s and 1970s, which forced peoples like the Hmong to migrate to the United States. Since then, federal immigration policies (see Chapter Two) have done much to increase the flow with their emphasis on family reunification. Yet the federal government has done little to provide funding or training for the teachers and administrators who are on the frontlines in the schools trying to "assimilate" these new Asian Americans into a culture that bears few similarities to those of their home countries.

The key problem obviously is that federal immigration policy has resulted in state government obligations. Indeed, passing the costs of newcomers onto the states after their initial resettlement appears to have been an explicit policy of the U.S. Congress (Hein, 1993, pp. 45–63). The federal government never expected communities, with their traditional local and state revenue base, to meet all of the costs of Southeast Asian refugees. Indeed, in 1977, the Social Security Administration Commissioner argued before the U.S. House of Representatives that "we have certain obligations . . . because of the war, and because they are new residents, to at least make this one-time attempt to give them a shot at being in the middle class, in the mainstream" (Hein, 1993, p. 78). By the mid 1980s, however, almost all financial and other responsibilities fell on state and local agencies—with only limited help from or connection with federal agencies.

It is inherently more expensive to educate non-English and limited-English speakers than to educate primary English speakers, because they require more time from the teacher to develop communication skills. Therefore, ideally they require smaller teacher-student ratios and more classrooms than monolingual English-speaking students. When there are few or no bilingual teachers who speak the students' home language, teachers require extensive in-service workshops and better pre-service preparation at universities. Specialized materials must also be developed and purchased for multicultural classrooms and school libraries. Although in the long run most immigrants and refugees pay their fair share of taxes (Fix and Passel, 1994), refugee families do not initially add to the property base of a community. Refugee families tend to move into the poorest neighborhoods, where schools are the most crowded and the least well equipped to handle new financial demands. Poor neighborhood schools are already dealing with a disproportionate share of other socially created problems, such as gangs, drug abuse, AIDS, unemployment, industrial decay, latchkey children, dysfunctional families, and multigenerational dependency on welfare.

In the final years of resettlement of Southeast Asian refugees, the Office of Refugee Resettlement did try to notify communities that they should budget for incoming Hmong refugee students, but the numbers predicted were often inaccurate. In general, limited funds for in-service workshops, lack of funding to purchase new materials, and inadequacy of classroom space have plagued schools in their attempts to meet the challenges of Southeast Asian immigrants since the late 1970s. This situation has forced states with Southeast Asian immigrant populations to divert money from other areas to schools, or it has increasingly resulted in overcrowded classrooms with inadequate resources and underprepared teachers. State bilingual funds and district funds were the usual sources of funding for new materials and rental of temporary classrooms. Local bond initiatives, when they were approved, have also paid for building additional classrooms. In California, additional school-district revenue has been derived from a state lottery. This has been used in a number of ways, including paying for in-service workshops in Rancho Centro.

The federal government has provided three potential sources of funding for educating refugee students: the Transitional Program for Refugee Children, the Emergency Immigration Education Act (EIEA), and Title VII of the Elementary and Secondary School Act, or the Bilingual Education Act. The Transitional Program for Refugee Children, also known as the Transitional Indochinese Refugee Act, ended with the 1989–90 school year. It provided a small amount of supplemental educational services for Southeast Asian refugee youngsters who had been in the United States for

fewer than three years. Although the funding for the EIEA has remained constant, the rapid increase in the number of immigrant
students resulted in a rapid decline of the amount allocated for
each student, from approximately $62 per student in 1989 to
approximately $36 in 1993 (Van Le, Office of Bilingual Education,
California Department of Education, Sacramento, California, conversation with author, April 13, 1994). Previously, funding was provided on the basis of numbers taken from the population census. To
be eligible for EIEA funding in 1993–94, a school district had to
have at least five hundred immigrant students, or those students had
to account for at least 3 percent of the district's total student population, and they had to have been attending schools in the United
States for less than three years. In most cases, the transitional and
emergency funds did not apply to areas of secondary migration, like
the Central Valley, where students had been in the United States
longer than three years. When refugee students have been in the
United States longer than three years, it is in the fiscal interest of
school districts to place as many students as possible in "bilingual
education" classes, where they become eligible for special state and
federal funds.

The third source of federal funding, Title VII, the Bilingual Education Act, is not an entitlement. It is a pool of funds, the size of
which is determined annually by Congress, and from which awards
are made competitively on a three-year basis to bilingual programs
based on need. Competition for Title VII grants is fierce, and annual
evaluations and efforts to renew them every three years have provided an incentive for educators to create truly outstanding
programs. Only two of the programs within Title VII, however,
allow for the participation of a large number (up to 40 percent) of
students who are bilingual but not categorized as LEP students. As
increasing numbers of Southeast Asian students enter mainstream
classrooms, all teachers, counselors, and administrators need the
kinds of programs available through Title VII grants.

Lack of Teacher Preparation

The basic challenge posed by large numbers of Hmong and other Southeast Asian students in classrooms is not their families' financial or formal educational limitations, or the influence of the home culture on student behavior. The problem is that teachers, administrators, and counselors lack preparation for dealing with their new students. Across the nation, the vast majority of teachers are European Americans and monolingual English speakers. As already mentioned, in states like California and New Mexico, and increasingly elsewhere, the majority of students are neither European American nor monolingual English speakers. In the spring of 1993, more than one million students, constituting 22 percent of the total enrollment in public schools in California, were classified as LEP.

The effectiveness of a teacher is severely compromised when he or she does not know how to learn about the home culture of a student and does not share the same primary language or socioeconomic background. Erickson (1986, p. 123) argued, "The teacher can be seen as a translator and as an intercultural broker. It is the teacher's responsibility to operate in such a bridging role on behalf of all students, regardless of the range of cultural diversity among students in a given classroom."

The lack of preparation of educators for teaching Southeast Asian students is evident at the most rudimentary levels. For example, even after more than ten years of teaching Southeast Asian students, many teachers and school administrators in Rancho Centro and Milltown still could not distinguish between different major ethnic groups, even when almost a quarter of their students were Southeast Asian. According to Micah Vang, "Teachers have had Hmong students for more than ten years, no Vietnamese, and they still think the Hmong are Vietnamese." Teachers call Vang and say, "There's a Vietnamese here who doesn't speak English. His name is Vue Vang." Vang is one of the ten most common Hmong clan names; it is not a Vietnamese name. This lack of sensitivity is widespread among teachers. In Seattle, a second-grade teacher proudly pointed to photographs on a bulletin board that she said showed "a Vietnamese New Year celebration" she had attended. The photographs were all of Mien mountain people from Laos wearing traditional clothing. The Mien are easily distinguishable from any other group because the women and girls wear thick red boas around their collars and heavily embroidered black turbans for special celebrations. The students in the teacher's class, like the Mien at the party, were too respectful to explain to her that they were not Vietnamese, and that, in fact, the Mien and Vietnamese are traditional enemies.

Teachers in Rancho Centro were also critical of administrators. One said, "The knowledge of administrators is shallow because that is their job, to know a little about a lot of things, but nothing in particular." An elementary school principal in Rancho Centro once earnestly asked how one can distinguish a Cambodian child from a Hmong child. The director of the Indochinese Advocacy Group in Milltown thought that most of the teachers could at least distinguish a Hmong from a Cambodian child; however, an advocate for refugees who runs a school for Southeast Asian women said, "The administration of Milltown school system, by and large, do not know. Maybe they can tell a Hmong from a Cambodian, but they cannot write five sensible sentences about their history, what brought them here, and what they are going through now."

In a 1987 survey, most teachers in Rancho Centro claimed that the educational needs of their students who were learning English were adequately met. Yet in the same survey almost half admitted that they had not received adequate education to effectively teach Southeast Asian students. Teachers in both Rancho Centro and Milltown often took contradictory positions regarding their preparation for teaching students who spoke other languages better than English. On the one hand, they described how they were doing a good job teaching these youngsters; but on the other, they admitted knowing nothing about their students' backgrounds or cultures.

In both Milltown and Rancho Centro there were no Southeast Asian classroom teachers. Both Rancho Centro and Milltown relied entirely on predominantly European descendants, monolingual English-speaking teachers, and there was little commitment on the part of either district, or their states' departments of education, or the U.S. Department of Education, to help Southeast Asian classroom aides and others become teachers. While it cannot be assumed that hiring a few Hmong teachers would help the Hmong, Hmong learn by observing and by doing, more so than most other peoples, because of their oral tradition. Including respected educated members of the Hmong community in the development of school initiatives would help schools to better understand and reach out to the community. They would also provide role models for Hmong youngsters.

University Preparation

Blame must certainly be placed on teacher preparation institutions and schools of education for failing to prepare teachers adequately for demographic changes in the classroom. All sixty-one teachers at a meeting in Rancho Centro in 1987 reported that they had at least one student categorized as LEP, but not one of the teachers had taken a college course that prepared them for teaching students from different cultural and language backgrounds than their own.

Although the need to understand other cultures has always existed in American schools, demographic changes in the 1980s augmented the need for cultural components in the preparation of educators. Many universities offer a generic multicultural education course. This may serve as an introduction, but it does not provide the depth of information that teachers need. Many universities offer courses on cultural psychology, history of immigrants, training in languages with different orthographies, and anthropology courses that cover oral traditions, animism, and other cultural influences on learning behavior, but they are not required of pre-service teachers, administrators, or counselors. The distinctions among Southeast Asians alone call for a special course.

The failure of schools of education to adequately prepare teachers for multicultural and multilingual classrooms means that teachers and administrators are often overwhelmed when confronted with one or many language or cultural groups in their classrooms. All students are affected, as teachers' available time and scarce resources are reallocated in an attempt to compensate for their lack of preparation.

Dr. Angel Sanchez of the County Office of Education in Los Angeles testified at the National Coalition of Advocates for Students hearing on immigrants in 1987: "At the public school level there is a pressing need to recruit teachers with the skills to reach and educate this diverse population of students. Teachers themselves should be acclimated to a changing pluralistic society. We'd like to see more teacher training by colleges and universities on strategies for dealing with culturally diverse students, and limited English proficient students. This means that colleges and universities need to attract and produce more teachers of diverse backgrounds and equip them with the skills necessary to meet the challenge of educating a diverse student population."

Need for Certified Bilingual Teachers

A primary problem facing school districts is the lack of certified bilingual teachers in many of the newcomer languages, including Hmong, Mien, Khmu, Lahu, Lao, Cambodian, and Vietnamese. The lack of Southeast Asian teachers will continue, according to an administrator in Seattle, "[because] we are not even preparing the kids we have" to go to college to become teachers.

Teacher preparation institutions and schools of education are just beginning to provide access to Southeast Asians interested in becoming teachers. The primary barrier to Hmong and other Southeast Asians entering the teaching profession is English syntax and the ability to write "nativelike" essays. Most Hmong students in college also need a counselor to advise them on courses. Joua Kue, described earlier, of the Milltown bilingual office, said:

There is no counselor to direct them to certain needs; they don't have people to advise them that this is good for you, that is good for you. That is the system. When they get to high school they already know that the English language will give them problems, so they go into a subject that is easier for them—engineering, computer science—where they find that whatever American kids can do, they can do. But, English, they have to have people helping them. They go to the class and listen to the teacher. They have to listen twice or three times.

A San Diego Community Schools experiment concluded that Hmong college students also need regular counselors, not necessarily Hmong, who speak English as a primary language. Twenty-five Vietnamese, Hmong, Lao, and Chinese Vietnamese began a San Diego program designed to help Southeast Asians who had been teachers in their native country to become teachers. In three years, the directors hoped that the Southeast Asians would complete their bachelor's degrees and fulfill the additional year of teacher education required in California. Although the program paid their tuition, no one completed the program in time. After several more years, a few graduated, but all had extreme difficulty passing the California Basic Educational Skills Test (CBEST) exams required of teachers. None of those who passed were Hmong.

The CBEST is a major hurdle faced by all Southeast Asians in California who want to become teachers. Such standardized tests are totally foreign to Hmong and others from oral traditions. Most of the test consists of multiple choice questions, including the math section, but the most difficult section is usually the essay section. Southeast Asians, like many foreign scholars, have extreme difficulty writing nativelike English. Teachers say they have particular problems with English syntax. These are issues that can be glossed over in spoken language, but show up unmistakably in written tests.

Joua Kue's story is an excellent example of how these general issues play out on an individual level. Joua's official title for twelve years in the bilingual office of the Milltown district schools was "home liaison." Kue benefited from a small Title VII grant in 1980 to Milltown district schools for a three-year program for Cambodians, Hmong, and Lao who said they had taught in the refugee camps of their first country and had teaching skills but no teaching credentials. Taking courses toward becoming a teacher was considered a career ladder. The grant paid for only part of the tuition at a local college and was intended to make Southeast Asians familiar with the American university system.

By 1989, Kue had more than half of the credits needed to complete a degree in elementary education or secondary school curriculum and become eligible for the state provisional elementary certificate or secondary school certificate. The provisional certificates are valid for six years. Kue was disappointed and angry that the Milltown school department was unable to help him pay for the rest of the credits he needed to complete his degree. In 1987, the local state college charged $81 per credit, or $199 for part-time students. As a "home liaison," Kue was earning a little over eight dollars an hour in 1986, and nine dollars an hour in 1989 after ten years of working on the same job. With three children, this salary was not sufficient to pay tuition. He wanted to become a teacher, but decided he could not afford to.

Another example of the lack of commitment to helping Southeast Asians become credentialed teachers is the story of a Lao aide. According to an elementary teacher who the aid worked with in Milltown, "She is marvelous. She knows the parents. She will go out and get the parents right in. She was a teacher in Laos. She's not really hired by the ESL office. She's a school aide. She speaks the language. She really should go back and get [her teaching credential.]" The principal and two teachers agreed that the Lao aide "could teach any class." Another teacher who had worked with her at the high school level said, "[She] was a mathematics teacher in her country who could whip out a calculus problem with any student. I begged [the local colleges] to help the girl; she has got to be a teacher. Total, total insensitivity on the part of the state. Someone should be slapped in the head."

The First Cambodian Resource Teacher

Sothit Ngor was the first Cambodian resource teacher hired by Milltown school district. Despite the enthusiasm in Milltown for hiring a Cambodian resource teacher, Sothit was very disillusioned about his position: "No matter what answer you get from Southeast Asian people, it won't work, because you have the public school department or political people." He added, "I don't think it's a problem of the teachers; the teacher is doing his job or her job everywhere. I admire that." Sothit Ngor hesitated and inhaled long and audibly before he said, "Probably it's a problem of local politics." He laughed the laugh of one who has seen the bear and knows he can do nothing about it.

Sothit continued to describe what it is like to be the first Cambodian "teacher" in the Milltown schools. Southeast Asians working in schools "have to know the privileges (of) time and input, (and be able to) teach," he said. His voice was stronger and angrier when he said, "Not just have those people come in and just order them. I'm thinking about teacher, personal counselor, or whatever. Not just to say, 'I need something' or 'stay after school' or to have those people translate. OK, I have to translate to the students and what the students say to me. They profit nothing! They don't know their feelings, they don't know what they really want. No matter what you try to get, you won't change anything. Not really change the system (to) make it profitable to the children."

The frustration in Sothit Ngor's voice and his description of his interactions with teachers, counselors, and other school department people reminded me of the way Americans and other foreigners treat interpreters in the refugee camps in Thailand: as if they are mindless. I asked Sothit if the role of Southeast Asians in the Milltown school was just like in the camps. Joua Kue was also there at the time. Both Sothit and Joua smiled. I had understood. One of them nodded, "Just like the camps."

In the first months of his new job, Sothit's responsibilities were to test elementary children for ESL placement at the central intake office. He visited schools, but he explained, "I don't really know what I have to do, to tell you the truth. But I went there and I asked the teachers to use me for whatever they'd like me to do. They use me to help with some students who have problems with language, like a tutor." There were no guidelines for resource teachers. After two years Sothit and the teachers had become accustomed to working together. Daily interaction improved Sothit's English and made him more empathetic toward the teachers. When he told them he would no longer be working in their classrooms, they expressed gratitude for all he had done and said they were sorry to see him go. "That wouldn't have happened two years ago," he said.

The Priority of Cultural Survival

This chapter has tried to make some sense of the scope of the challenge facing the U.S. public education system. The challenge in educating new immigrant students includes better preparation for existing teachers to learn about the unfamiliar cultures and the family backgrounds of their students, and to work effectively with primary-language resource teachers and aides in the classroom. It also includes the need to provide career ladders for classroom aides to become bilingual teachers, funding to support their endeavors, and college-level counselors to provide the support that potential teachers' aides need to make it through the system. If educators in Rancho Centro and Milltown had been provided with even the most basic information on the backgrounds of their incoming students they would have handled their situations much better. As one teacher explained, they did not even know what questions to ask.

The primary failing of both Milltown's and Rancho Centro's responses to the Hmong is that they did not attempt to integrate the Hmong community into the educational community. A wealth of interest and commitment was not tapped. They failed to reach out to parents, community leaders, and the students themselves. As a result, the Hmong themselves have very little role in the schools. Vang's experience was exceptional; but he was accepted by teachers as a valid source of information because he had a French education, not because he was Hmong.

The issue that teachers in Milltown and Rancho Centro most needed to understand, which will be taken up in the next chapter, was the Hmong cultural priority for survival. Most teachers experienced this on an immediate and material basis, by trying to teach newly arrived children about American dress codes and how to get around the school buildings; but the teachers were so busy trying to survive themselves in their new situation that they failed to grasp the enduring significance of giving priority to cultural survival. Survival is not a temporary priority that will end once children learn how to dress like other students and where to find the toilets. Vang said that every Hmong knows the American teachers need to understand Hmong culture and the fact that retaining Hmong culture is the top priority of the Hmong. "But no one says anything. Who is going to fight for that?" Vang asks. "The Hmong may be proud, but they are only refugees."

∞∞ 4

Culture and Learning

There is a tendency in the academic literature, particularly in U.S.-based studies of Hmong refugee resettlement, to make broad programmatic statements about Hmong culture. The literature on the Hmong in Thailand, Laos, and China suggests instead that flexibility is an important aspect of Hmong culture. Writing about Hmong who settled in northern Thailand many decades ago, Geddes (1976, p. 72) determined that "relationships are constantly being varied according to contemporary circumstances. In the migratory way of life the younger generations are the pioneers and therefore the new relationships they make become the focal points of new alignments, convenience in the present being of greater importance in many cases than association in the past."

The norms of immigrant behavior in general, and Hmong behavior in particular, belong to lives vastly different from the life familiar to most American communities; and for young Hmong, as well as for other children of immigrants in the United States, these norms also belong to a world that no longer exists except in the behavior of their elders. For many older Hmong, the norms of behavior that came with them from their country of origin constitute reality, and these older Hmong often regard their life here as temporary. The same is true of many other older immigrants. This generational tension between two opposing views on life in the United States poses a serious challenge for schools trying to connect home and school learning. It also poses a serious challenge for the family culture.

In this chapter I turn to a discussion of how culture influences learning. I explain the importance of cultural identity and explore how cultural identity and cultural priorities challenge motivation theory, particularly in terms of gender roles that dictate certain types of behavior, and I examine how the demand to survive in American schools creates a tension among these priorities.

A Mountain People

For Hmong culture to survive its encounter with American public schools, Hmong children must integrate old scripts with new scripts. Some are not sure the Hmong are ready to merge their culture with American culture. Micah Vang, introduced in Chapter Three, who was educated in France and received a master's degree from California State University, explained that there are

> so many theories, I'm not sure the Hmong agree. To be Hmong or to be completely assimilated to our Western culture, that is the thought of so many Hmong. They never ask, but when you see the evolution of the culture, changing of the lifestyle, their physical mind, their mental mind and their body, their behavior are not ready at all for the assimilation, [to be] integrated, but we worry [that] they have to change themselves to the mainstream, but they are not ready at all, they do not know anything about that.

Nevertheless, Hmong leaders like Vang believe in the value of integration; they believe that Hmong students must prove they are the equal of American students. It is better for Hmong students to work their way up from the bottom, Vang says. "When they come from the bottom to the top, you don't have any argument, they're just [equal]."

Outsiders may not understand the Hmong unless they recognize the importance of a strong group identity and the role that identity plays in the ordering of Hmong daily life. One reason the Hmong have survived thousands of years of change, from the "backside of China" to the United States, is that there is a Hmong ethos, an understanding that the Hmong must work together to survive. Vang claims that only one Hmong ever betrayed another Hmong, "and he was not really Hmong." "The Hmong are born into a collective relationship," he says, and in this relationship the group takes precedence over the individual. In Laos when someone needed a house, "everyone helps to build without asking, never pay, hope to pay back with own labor." A Hmong man in Chico, California, explained that the collective identity is so strong in the United States that when a Hmong arrives in a new area, he just looks for another Hmong for a place to stay and help getting settled. In Southeast Asia, kinship ties were very important, but in the United States it no longer matters if the two are members of the same clan.

The Hmong, like the Mien, Khmu, Lahu, and Lua', are a mountain people; Cambodians, Laotians, and Vietnamese are not. This distinction is similar to that between Native American populations and the Europeans who came to settle on this continent. The Hmong and other mountain people, like many Native Americans, share an identity that has often been called "tribal"; but the word "tribal" has lost its value because it was used in Africa to denigrate the political coherence of nations of people (Barbara Harrell-Bond, Refugee Studies Programme, Oxford University, communication with author, June 21, 1994).

An advocate for refugees in Milltown suggested that the reason the Hmong have maintained a unified front against the aggressions of war and continued to identify as a coherent group—unlike the Cambodians, for example, who submitted to the whims of the Khmer Rouge and sometimes became the enemy in order to survive—"has something to do with the strong family unit that came intact with the Hmong. Where there's been so much genocide with the Cambodians that most are surviving alone, or just with a very few family members. Look at the young adults who came here with nobody."

A Cambodian resource teacher in Milltown explained how the Cambodians never had "extended families, even in our country." Compared to the Hmong culture, "the teachings or the philosophies are different," he said. One high school teacher in Milltown tried to understand why more of his Cambodian male students than Hmong students dropped out of school, carried knives and "chute sticks," and had "totally belligerent attitudes." He explained:

> I could understand all of the psychological implications, the kids are alone in the house, coming to school with a survival mentality, a little ticked off about what was going on, why the Hmong were driving around with brand new cars, you know, "I'm an immigrant, too, refugee." The whole system, they had a system, the Laotians and Hmong, and that was the community organizations, and that was fantastic. If you had a problem, let it go into the community and it will come back very shortly, resolved. If the parents couldn't handle it, the community, the leaders would handle it. The Cambodians had no one to go to. Mainly because factions in the adults are unbelievably strong.

Hmong identity is based on the clan system. There were approximately twenty-five original clans in Laos, and there are ten that are common in the United States. Yang Dao (1992, p. 288), the senior Hmong scholar and one of the first to earn a doctorate, explained that "children are members of their father's clan and take its name. The clan is made up of a male ancestor, his sons and unmarried daughters, and the children of his sons presumably going back 160 or more generations. . . . When Hmong left Thai refugee camps, they adopted their clan names as their last names."

Kinship terms used by clan members reflect the importance of

the clan relationship to men and the role of women in clan relationships. Uncles and male cousins of the same generation are
called "older brother" or "younger brother." Older male relatives are
referred to as "older father" or "younger father." Yang (1992)
explained:

> People who are related to one another through an
> unbroken male line of descent are called *kwv tij*, or patri-
> lineal relatives. The two words characterize the rela-
> tionship: *kwv* ("younger brother") and *tij* ("older
> brother"). The lineage group, or *caj ceg* ("branch" and
> "root"), includes brothers, their sons, and male grand-
> children—all of the males in each generation going back
> as far as memory allows. Members of the same genera-
> tion call each other *kwv* or *tij*, while their children refer
> to them as *txiv* ("father"), *txiv hlb* ("older father") or *tsiv
> ntxawm* ("younger father"). They have specific duties
> towards one another and they share the same ancestral
> spirits traced to an original male founder of the lineage
> group." [1992, p. 290]

The *kwv tij* relationship is extended to Hmong with the same
clan name, even though there is no blood relationship (Yang, 1992,
p. 290). Thao (1986) points out that a fellow clan member can
expect shelter and assistance from any other member of the clan,
even if they have never known of one another before; but as Yang
(1992, p. 290) pointed out, "If their sense of clan membership is
not strong, their obligations toward one another are vague and
often weak, and their duties are limited to occasional visits and
assistance."

Women have no power in the clan system, except if they come
from a strong family that forms a strong alliance with the *kwv tij*. A
woman's most important role is to form alliances between clans
through marriage and to propagate her husband's clan with many

male children. The special term for those related to a man through his wife, mother, grandmother, the wife of his son, or the wife of his grandson is *neejtsa*. According to Yang (1992, pp. 290–91), "There is no English equivalent term, and "relatives-in-law" is not exactly right. In the Western way, "in-laws" would include the brother's wife. In the Hmong kinship system, the brother's wife is not an in-law, because she becomes an integral part of her husband's family, adopting his ancestor spirits as her own. Her relatives, however, are *neejtsa*." Marriage within an exogamous clan is regarded as incestuous.

Leadership in the clan system is strictly hierarchical and patrilineal. Yang (1985, p. 4) claims that it was the sense of security provided by the clan system, "founded on a millennium of solidarity, (that) has been able through the centuries to help the Hmong avoid juvenile delinquency, begging and other social evils." Ironically, it appears that the group identity has recently begun to lend itself to gang membership, at least for some Hmong (Ima, 1992). The innate clan identity may make gang development and a sense of peer identity particularly appealing to young Hmong who feel that their elders are irrelevant as role models in the United States.

The recent rise in juvenile delinquency among Hmong adolescents suggests that the sense of security provided by the Hmong clan system no longer meets the demands of survival in American streets and schools, and that some youths are turning to their peers instead of to their elders and extended family for security. The implications are profound. As Hmong begin to accommodate the importance placed on the individual in school and elsewhere in the United States in order to succeed in American society, the Hmong patrilineal authority structure breaks down. With it goes the clan system and the traditional sense of security that has given young Hmong the confidence to become model citizens. Efforts are now being made in the Hmong community by former military leaders and respected educated men to redefine or reassert the traditional authority system.

While the clan system appears to be shaken by its encounter with American youth culture, the group identity and cooperative learning strategies (discussed later in this chapter) of Hmong students are still strong. In research on Hmong high school students in St. Paul and Minneapolis in the early 1980s, Sonsalla (1984) found that the cultural identity of Hmong students led to a different set of priorities than those of their American teachers. He concluded that the highest priority of Hmong students was to preserve their culture. This clashed with the highest priority of American teachers, which was to assimilate the Hmong. The theory of survival introduced later in this chapter argues that the highest priority of Hmong students is not necessarily the *preservation* of their culture, but the *survival* of their culture. Cultural survival requires flexibility, not preservation.

Bringing Culture to School

It is a most important fact that Hmong students do not leave behind their culture when they walk into an American classroom. Even if they were born in the United States, their identity is a group identity and their learning style is derived from an oral tradition. Because of the strong group identity, Hmong students are skilled in the group learning process, commonly called cooperative learning.

Cooperative Learning

Goldstein (1985, p. 261) wrote that Hmong youth are "socialized to a world view in which the group took precedence over the individual, and personal well-being was dependent on the health of the family or kin group." Jenny Dailey, the principal of the elementary school in Rancho Centro introduced in Chapter Three, provided one example of how Hmong students help each other. She often stood at the beginning of the lunch line in the school cafeteria with a checklist of students who received free federally subsidized lunches because their families lived below the poverty level. Often, a

Hmong would put his face right next to a new Hmong child's mouth and say the child's name like a puppeteer. He would do this for two reasons: so the principal would not realize the newcomer did not understand English, and so the newcomer would learn what to do. In a class for Hmong aides in Rancho Centro, Hmong adults would answer questions under their breath to help each other. It is as if, when one asks one Hmong a question, one really asks all Hmong. In one fifth grade class in Rancho Centro, two Hmong girls sat at the back of the room, sharing a desk and discussing their work. Typical of the division of labor by gender and of cultural taboos, Hmong girls work only with other girls, boys only with other boys. Other students, however, resented the Hmong students being allowed to work together.

On the one hand, from the Hmong perspective cooperative learning means that bright students are able to help slower students, so that the students advance as a group. On the other hand, the cooperative learning style may partially explain the difficulty Hmong have with standardized tests, which has been well documented by Rumbaut and Ima (1987). Since birth, Hmong have learned to work with others rather than as individuals. The idea of sitting down at a desk and writing answers on a piece of paper without discussing the problem is un-Hmong. Furthermore, it is wrong in Hmong culture to compete with other Hmong. In her study of the learning of Hmong adults in Madison, Wisconsin, Hvitfeldt (1986, p. 70) found that cooperation, noncompetitiveness, and group support were "central to the Hmong students' interpretation of student role." Students denied any individual ability, even when they were personally praised by the teacher. Hvitfeldt explained that "individual students are continuously in touch with those around them, maintaining interpersonal interaction through verbal and nonverbal checking of each other's books, papers and worksheets. The weaker students look around for assurance; the stronger students maintain a constant check on the work of the weaker students in order to make certain that they are progressing correctly. Help is freely given, and even when not requested, accepted as a matter of course" (p. 70). It is wrong to compete with fellow Hmong. Given the opportunity, Hmong in school work best in cooperative situations in which they can analyze problems together and share answers.

The cooperative learning style accounts for the loneliness Hmong students experience when they are placed in college-track schools or in classes with no other Hmong. A fourteen-year-old Hmong boy felt lonely because he was the only Hmong in his seventh grade class. "Americans see you, but they don't notice you," he said. A Hmong man said he felt isolated and lonely as a result of having been well educated. He could not talk to his wife or brother. When he returned to his family after studying in Vientiane, the capitol of Laos, he did not know how to do the things other Hmong knew how to do. He did not know how to fish, and he did not know the songs for the courtship ball-throwing ritual at the New Year's celebration. He could only talk, and that was boring for the girls. "You can never go back completely. I feel like I don't fit into any situation. [You] try to be elite. Elite what? For how long? I am so isolated, so really lonely," he explained.

The problems faced by Hmong intellectuals are not unique; immigrants from other ethnic groups have faced similar difficulties. According to a Pakistani who taught in Rancho Centro, "the more you are in education or the urban world, the less [your own people] trust you—it's a double-edged sword." Writing about Polish peasant immigrants at the turn of the century, Thomas and Znaniecki (1984, pp. 217–218) discussed the problem of alienation faced by the individual who learns to read in a nonreading community: "[He] has interests which the community does not share, ideas which differ from those of others, and information which others cannot obtain, he isolates himself in some measure from his environment and lives partly in a sphere which is inaccessible to others and—what is worse—strange and unknown to them; thus, he in certain respects breaks away from social control." They argued that "the development of intellectual interests is closely connected with breakdown of the isolation of the peasant community and the consequent disorganization of the old system." This is inevitable, they claimed, because "growing contact with the outside world develops in the individuals a desire for new experiences."

Gee (1986) argued that as children from preliterate societies become literate, their identity with their group will change, because the ways in which a people converse "are tied to their particular world views." This finding suggests that as individual Hmong become more educated, they will become more independent from the group—less Hmong. Whether or not Hmong culture survives American education depends on how the Hmong use their education.

Some Hmong are trying to preserve their language for social and cultural interaction. When I wanted a Hmong translation of a farm proposal I wrote at the Ban Vinai refugee camp in Thailand, three translators tried to oblige me. Finally, the third, the most skilled at translating culture, explained that the Hmong used Lao, not Hmong, to write accounts of business affairs. Today, most young Hmong who do not know Lao or Thai use English for academic and business purposes. Of course, this practice excludes many Hmong women who do not read in any language, but who could understand if someone read them something in Hmong.

Oral Tradition

A force mitigating against preservation of the Hmong language for social and cultural interaction is that as the Hmong become educated and literate, they will have less time to spend learning their oral traditions. If traditional Hmong stories and beliefs are to survive formal education, it may be necessary to write them down. More and more Hmong are now learning to read and write in Hmong. It is said that only a few weeks are required to learn the system if one knows the Hmong language and how to write in any other language. It is possible that literacy will destroy the Hmong group identity; but my guess is that literacy is coming with so many other changes that the stories of the oral tradition will be unrecognizable in the future. That is the beauty of oral tales, however; the same tale is never told twice.

The Hmong have recorded Hmong history since the last war in Southeast Asia along with their animistic tales in the embroidery of storycloths by women. These cloths are a variation on the traditional *pun dtao*—the brilliantly colored reverse appliqué squares for which Hmong women are known. In the refugee camps of Thailand, the storycloths and *pun dtao* reached a high art. The women were equipped with thread and cloth sold to them by Thai villagers, and they found a market among camp volunteers and traders from Thai tourist towns. The market for these pieces of art escalated in the early 1980s. In the late 1980s, however, the Thai government clamped down on the marketing of goods inside the refugee camps, especially handicrafts that earned refugees more income than local Thai farmers could earn from their rice crops. Since coming to the United States, however, many Hmong women no longer have time to sew.

Embroidery and the rural lifestyle of most Southeast Asians encouraged the development of a high degree of eye-hand coordination and, consequently, the early development of fine motor skills. Computer industries in Boulder, Colorado, and Lowell, Massachusetts, among other places, have capitalized on this talent, hiring many Southeast Asians, particularly women. Such skills also show up in school. Sally Fulton, introduced in Chapter Three as an elementary school principal in Rancho Centro, said that

[Hmong] children have extremely well-developed fine motor skills. I don't know if this is environmental—in the home they're taught to use their fingers at a very early age, but their handwork, their handwriting. When they are taught something it is beautiful. When they first start, they don't know what to do. When you show them how to do it, they do a wonderful job. Their penmanship is usually neat and precise. Far superior to our children. Of course they're already a year older. Very little of the random scribbling you see among four- and five-year-olds in our culture. I know it's a developmental thing, so they must give their kids things to do with their hands early.

In Laos and in the refugee camps the Hmong did not benefit from the products of industrial society. Beginning at age three, girls learned the intricate stitching needed to make *pun dtao* and story-cloths. Almost everything had to be made by hand. Fields were cultivated by hand; water was drawn by hand (except when it could be piped in using systems of split bamboo), and food was cooked over an open stove. Unfortunately, the tradition of embroidery and the skills that are developed along with it are dying because children now attend school and no longer have the time or patience to learn them.

Hmong oral tradition and the history of the Hmong as a language minority seem to give the Hmong advantages when learning to speak other languages. Teachers have found that verbal messages are better understood than written ones. Hmong seem to learn languages much as children learn their first language—by listening and imitating. A Milltown teacher was amazed at how her Southeast Asian elementary students "seem to pick up the vocabulary and the reading in an untaught way, in a more natural way. In other words, they begin to identify words like 'dinosaur' because they've seen it so much, I guess." Actually, it is probably the early memory training of the Hmong that the teacher is observing.

The oral tradition gives the Hmong early training in memorization. One kindergarten teacher in Stockton, California, told how Hmong students in her class memorized her roster every year in alphabetical order and took attendance for her every morning. A Rancho Centro Title VII instructor found that Hmong children were memorizing what they heard and reciting instead of reading.

This becomes a problem after the third grade when children cannot memorize everything and are forced into remedial programs, he said. Mien adults, who also come from an oral tradition, also sometimes memorize instead of reading.

Rumbaut and Weeks (1986) found that despite rural origins and lower levels of education, a smaller percentage of Hmong could not speak any English compared to the Cambodian, Chinese Vietnamese, and lowland Lao refugees. The Hmong oral tradition and their history as a language minority seem to give them advantages in learning to speak another language by training their auditory memories. It seems logical that if the learning style of the Hmong relies on hearing and listening, teachers ought to link these auditory strengths to learning how to read and write.

The Kamehameha Early Language Program, developed in Hawaii, was based on just such a strategy. It concentrated on incorporating the native Hawaiian method of cooperative storytelling into the curriculum. In doing so, it regarded the skills developed by the oral tradition as strengths rather than handicaps. As a result, the reading scores of native, Creole-speaking Hawaiians increased from about the fifteenth percentile to a medium range between the fortieth and seventy-fifth percentile in grades one through three (Cummins 1984; Robert Kovats, letter to author, March 1989).

Two aspects of Hmong oral tradition may run counter to Western logic. In Hmong culture, a sharp distinction does not exist between fiction and nonfiction. Hmong parables mix fact and fiction. The failure to understand this aspect of Hmong culture caused problems for Hvitfeldt (1986). Hvitfeldt's adult Hmong students persisted in asking detailed questions about fictional characters, as if the characters lived nearby. Hvitfeldt interpreted these questions to mean that the Hmong thought the fictional characters were living people. In fact, Hmong folktales contain many fictional characters, and they believe that these fictional characters interact with living characters and spirits.

A second aspect of Hmong culture that surprises Westerners is the genuine sense of humor that is almost always maintained in Hmong stories, no matter how sad or gruesome. Both are illustrated by a story told by a Hmong man named Kue Pao, who I first met in Ban Vinai. Kue Pao often told stories that began with a situation we both knew, but then left me totally lost, usually in the world of animistic spirits. For example, he explained that the Hmong at Ban Vinai refugee camp were not concerned about goiter because if a person with goiter slept on top of a new grave, a spirit would come and take the goiter away to use as a cooking pan. If the spirit wanted to return the goiter but could not find the person he had taken it from, the spirit would give it to someone else.

Emergence of Lags in Skill Development

Most of the Hmong and other Laotian mountain children now in the U.S. schools do not remember life in Laos. Most were born in refugee camps or are native-born Americans. In recent years some kindergarten and first grade Hmong and Mien students appear to be lagging behind others in the development of memory skills, motor skills, eye-hand coordination, and time-on-task skills. This comes as a surprise to teachers who had Hmong and other Laotian students ten years ago who were very advanced in all of these areas, but it is not inexplicable in light of the fact that the traditional means of developing these skills—participation in oral rituals, embroidery, and silver work—are no longer being taught to children in the home. Most Hmong and other rural parents also are not teaching these skills the way many other American families do—with crayons and coloring books, scissors, and cut-outs, and by reading to their children nightly.

"What has emerged after ten years of classroom work with the children of these groups is that oral English skills can be excellent while reading skills lag far behind," wrote Judy Lewis in a September 1990 newsletter of the Southeast Asia Community Resource Center at Folsom Cordova Unified School District. The reason reading skills lag far behind oral skills is that there are few, if any, reading materials in most Laotian homes. Generally speaking, there are no newspapers, books, magazines, or other written information besides those brought home by students. It is interesting to note that in most cases the books and papers brought home by students are treated almost reverentially, and kept out of reach of younger siblings.

Classroom Participation

A two-way cultural misunderstanding is responsible for the lack of Hmong participation in the classroom. For example, many Hmong students are reluctant to speak in class because they are shy and embarrassed about their English pronunciation. It is also not culturally acceptable for girls to be aggressive verbally or physically. Hmong culture prizes shyness among Hmong girls. At the same time, Hmong students, boys and girls, complain to their elders that they are not very challenged in their classrooms.

As can be seen in related studies among other groups, cultural shyness may not be the only issue. Susan Phillips found that on the Warm Springs Indian Reservation in central Oregon the silence and nonparticipation of Native American children in traditional classrooms could be explained by the fact that "the social conditions for participation to which they have become accustomed in the Indian community are lacking" (Cazden, Carrasco, Maldonado-Guzman, and Erickson, 1980, p. 64). An elementary school teacher in Milltown told me she felt that Hmong are more difficult to teach than Cambodians because they are quiet. In the French school system in Laos, students never dared ask questions of the teachers. Girls learned by staying at home, asking mother, grandmother, neighbors—but never strangers. The cadence of the Hmong communication is slower and more rhythmic than that of English. Often I was struck by the lilting voices that greeted me as I entered Ban Vinai. Hmong will often wait to speak until after a long silence in order to show respect for the previous speaker. Americans do not recognize how these empty spaces in conversation are really part of the conversation. There is a tendency to cut off a Hmong person just before they are about to speak.

Nonverbal signals are usually a Hmong student's way of saying he or she would like to speak. Teachers are often unable to recognize these signs. As a result, they fail to call on Hmong or Mien students who may want to be called on, teased, and challenged like other students. Tracy, a Mien high school student in northern California said, "They treat Asians different. Teachers think Asians don't understand because they're quiet. They don't pick on them—have to raise hand. Don't fool around or joke with Asians. They think Asians are different."

One result of not speaking up is that teachers sometimes think Hmong students understand when they do not. A Hmong girl in Milltown told me that teachers ignore her because she does not speak English well and they do not speak Hmong. The mother of a preschool Mien student in northern California told me, "Her teachers don't know that she understands, but doesn't know how to answer." Her older sister, a fourth grader, said she can tell that some teachers do not like Mien because they never talk to them or pick them when they raise their hands. I once observed a classroom in Colorado in which a young Hmong girl thought she was raising her hand when she only waved it slightly beside her desk. The teacher was surprised later when I asked why he had not called on the girl. He said he had not seen her hand.

Motivation Theory and the Hmong

Much current debate about the success of certain ethnic and linguistic minority students and the failure of others has focused on the issue of motivation. Motivation theories explain that the reason certain minority students perform poorly in school, misbehave, and finally drop out is that they lack adequate motivation. The motivation debate fits nicely into the context of Asian American academic success. Theorists may simply argue that Asian American students are "motivated," while Native American, African American, and Latino American students are not. However, analyses of differences in motivation among ethnic groups are often conducted without regard for important internal differences of class, gender, culture, and language.

Most research on motivation theory leaves unanswered questions about the source of academic motivation. Proposed answers to these questions can generally be divided into two schools of thought, one stressing events internal to the classroom and the other stressing external events. Events internal to the classroom that motivate or alienate a student may result from similarities or differences between the teacher and the student in terms of expectations, communication styles, learning styles, language usage, and norms of behavior (Erickson, 1987). Ogbu (1978, 1987, 1990) has been the preeminent exponent of the theory of events external to the classroom. He has claimed that the history and background of students is the most important factor shaping academic motivation. Ogbu (1987) has also distinguished between "voluntary" immigrants and "involuntary" minorities. Among the latter group are slaves from Africa, relocated Native Americans, and the original Mexican inhabitants of today's southwestern United States. According to Ogbu, involuntary minorities have been jaded by past unsuccessful experiences, and they are not motivated to succeed in school because of job ceilings and a history of inferior education. "While cultural, language and opportunity barriers are very important for all minorities, the main factor differentiating the more successful from the less successful minorities appears to be the nature of the history, subordination and exploitation of the minority, and the nature of the minority's own instrumental and expressive responses to the treatment, which enter into the process of their schooling" (p. 317).

Theoretically, the Hmong paradigm demonstrates that events both internal and external to the classroom influence a group's academic motivation in American schools. Because the Hmong arrived so recently, with no group history in this country, the experiences of Hmong students enable to some extent the making of distinctions between the cultural influences of the United States on a minority group and the cultural influences that predate their lives here. These distinctions cannot be made with African Americans, the majority of whom first crossed the Atlantic Ocean prior to the 1770s (Curtain, 1990, p. 21). Nor can they be made with Latino or Native American peoples, most of whom predate Europeans in this part of the world. It is also difficult to distinguish the cultural influences on Chinese, Japanese, or other Asian Americans, even though the majority have come since 1965, because their ancestors began coming to the United States in the 1800s.

The vigor that Hmong exhibit in American schools is based on a shared belief that survival in the United States depends on academic success. (Chapter One defined Hmong vigor as being highly motivated despite extreme poverty, uneducated parents, and having few Hmong role models who have achieved financial or academic success.) The struggle for survival is a particularly strong academic motivation for some Hmong boys. In accordance with the Hmong patrilineal authority system, many still follow the dictates of their Vietnam War–era leader, General Vang Pao, who told them to get as much education during their sojourn in the United States as they could so that they could bring knowledge back with them when they return to Laos. Although the departure of Soviet advisers from Laos, and the repatriation from Thailand to Laos of Hmong who did not qualify for resettlement in the United States, makes the return of the Hmong more realistic, most of the young Hmong Americans are no longer interested in returning. For many, the motivation to return to Laos has been superseded by their new identity as Americans and by a few well-known Hmong scholar role models who encourage Hmong to study for the sake of knowledge. (This group of exceptional individuals have joined together to form a national committee called Hmong National Development, which is committed to developing the self-sufficiency of Hmong and to improving their educational opportunities.)

Most Hmong students appear to be successful because they are highly motivated and are rewarded with high grade point averages; but as explained in Chapter One, grade point averages can be misleading. The reality is that Hmong "success" is generally due to the fact that the majority are placed in ESL and low-level, non-college-bound classes. Hmong students also tend to have higher grade point averages than most other students because of the relevance of education to their cultural priorities for survival in the United States; but they have lower-than-average standardized test scores, because, as explained earlier, the skills taught in their home culture are irrelevant when it comes to standardized testing procedures.

Since Hmong youngsters first arrived in American classrooms around 1981, teachers have commented that Hmong youngsters are model students—that they are polite, eager, and respectful, and that they do their homework neatly and on time. Recently, however, teachers have begun to see changes in Hmong students' behavior. While most Hmong students continue to be models of "correct" behavior, more and more Hmong youngsters are acting like other school children: skipping school, hanging out at shopping malls, and giving priority to being regarded as "cool" by their fellow students. Changes in Hmong children's behavior at school implies that their cultural scripts are changing. They are no longer just Hmong. They are Hmong Americans.

As mentioned earlier, there has recently been a rise in juvenile delinquency among Hmong boys that appears to be gang-related (Ima, 1992). Perhaps this is partly the result of Hmong youngsters becoming disillusioned with school when they realize that the education they worked so hard for does not qualify them for the type of skilled or white-collar jobs they envisioned—or even enable them to apply to a four-year college. Perhaps their gang affiliations are a reaction to the realization that school replaces their cultural identity with a new minority identity that has limited their opportunities in a racist environment. If this is the case, this would be in contrast to the argument that immigrants succeed academically because they "[do not] define school learning as an instrument for replacing their cultural identity with the cultural identity of their 'oppressors' without full reward or assimilation" (Ogbu, 1987, p. 334). My own findings suggest that the rise of Hmong gangs is the result of their traditional group identity responding to the rules of survival for adolescent minorities in poor American communities.

A strong group identity is in part derived in response to external pressures on a group's survival. As has been shown in this chapter, the Hmong group identity takes precedence over the members' identities as individuals. This might lead one to expect that Hmong academic performance will deteriorate; academic motivation has often been inversely related to peer pressure, on the assumption that peer pressure prevents students from trying to succeed. Fordham and Ogbu (1986) found that African American students sometimes discourage academic achievement among their peers by referring to it as "acting white."

Group identity does not in itself have a negative effect on academic motivation. The urban Vietnamese, many of whom typify the myth of the "amazing Asian American," have long had a strong oppositional identity. An oppositional identity enabled the Vietnamese to oust the Chinese after a thousand years of occupation, to withstand French colonialism for a hundred years, and to defeat the United States in a relatively brief but devastating war. The strength of this oppositional identity is still evident in the United States. Vietnamese youngsters frequently talk about "us" and "them," where "them" refers to all other Americans, be they European American, African American, Latino, or members of other Asian American groups. Vietnamese youngsters demonstrate that groups can maintain an oppositional identity even while succeeding at school.

Many Southeast Asians do not intend to give up their cultural identity. Like other immigrants before them, Southeast Asian parents assume that their home language and cultural identity can be maintained at home while children are learning at school to survive in the United States. In retrospect, this perspective appears naive, and reflects little familiarity with the forces of assimilation. The rise of gangs and the increase of typical American behavior among Hmong students indicates that the way youngsters are learning to survive in school is not what parents had in mind. Differences between Hmong parents' norms of behavior and their children's behavior reflects the differences between the material and social demands for survival in Laos and those in the United States.

The Hmong paradigm challenges the importance of motivation as a predictor of academic success. Motivation may be irrelevant when cultural priorities—such as early child rearing among school-age Hmong girls to ensure the biological survival of the Hmong— take precedence over academic aspirations. Motivation also may not matter when a group is consistently placed in low-level, non-college-track classes based solely on standardized test scores.

Cultural influences on learning behavior, rather than the influence of socioeconomic or educational background, best explain Hmong performance in American schools; but cultural influences clearly cut both ways. On the one hand, they result in a high level of motivation—where motivation has not been rendered irrelevant by other cultural priorities. On the other hand, they hamper Hmong access to high-level, college-track classes. The result is that Hmong students appear to be doing very well when in fact their success comes only at the lowest rungs of the academic ladder.

A Theory of Survival

All children bring into the classroom cultural scripts modeled on the material and social environments in which their parents have lived. Cultural scripts reflect the cultural priorities and norms of behavior by which a group distinguishes itself from others. The norms of behavior of immigrant and refugee students are vastly different from those that govern the behavior of most American students, regardless of class or race. Class and gender, however, frame the educational options open to all youngsters. In order to succeed academically, newcomer students' own particular blend of cultural priorities must allow them to integrate old scripts with new scripts.

Greer (1972, p. 91) wrote: "What the child brings with him to the public school classroom is not a pure or direct product of an historic land of origin, but the combined product of some of those patterns and the patterns established by the group in order to survive in the place assigned to it in America." The need for teachers to understand the survival strategies, cultures, and backgrounds of their students is especially true for the Hmong because their culture is so different from mainstream middle-class American culture.

The struggle to survive has been, and continues to be, the key to Hmong ethnicity, and it is a repeating pattern in Hmong oral history. Survival, as a trait of the Hmong culture, became pronounced as a result of continual threats from the outside. The struggle for survival marks all immigrants, especially refugees; but the Hmong were forced to fight for their survival long before they became involved in the war in Laos in the 1960s alongside the United States. The Hmong have always been a minority at odds with the existing powers; and they have often been forced to move in order to preserve their cultural identity. The Hmong oral history says that this nomadism is part of their second phase of existence. In the first phase, the Hmong believe, they had their own country; but after they lost their country they became downtrodden and were forced to unify to advance themselves. Eventually, the Hmong hope to become free of any foreign domination.

Many Hmong from Laos remember personally that the threat to Hmong survival was intensified during the 1960s and 1970s when a great number of Hmong died fighting as mercenaries in the U.S.-funded war against communism. The Hmong paid a significant price for their role in this war. In the last seven years of fighting, from 1967 through 1975, 70 percent of new recruits were between 10 and 16 years of age (Mottin, 1980, p. 52). In 1968, Edgar Buell, known as "Pop Buell," an operative for the U.S. Special Forces in Laos, reported to *The New Yorker*, "A short time ago we rounded up 300 fresh recruits. Thirty percent were 14 years old or less, and 10 of them were only 10 years old. Another 30 percent were 15 or 16. The remaining 40 percent were 45 or older. Where are the ones in between? I'll tell you—they're all dead" (McCoy, Reed and Adams, 1972, p. 281). A report to the Senate Judiciary Subcommittee on Refugees and Escapees in 1970 estimated that 50 percent of the total population of four hundred thousand Hmong in Laos were killed by the war. An estimated 90 percent of the villagers in the north were affected by the bombing (Rickenbach, 1970).

The Hmong, Mien, and other mountain people were forced to leave disease-free mountain villages and move to malaria-ridden lowland areas. As the bombing intensified, these mountain people hid in the jungles, where they existed on banana leaves, roots, and tree bark. Most of the babies died, as did many of the elders who could not digest such food. Unfamiliar with large bodies of water, and having drugged their babies with opium to prevent them from crying, the Hmong lost more babies in the Mekong River. Consequently, there is tremendous cultural pressure on Hmong women to reproduce as often as possible. And they do.

Women in Hmong Culture

Hmong norms of behavior reflect the importance the Hmong have placed on their survival as a people. In particular, they have a profound impact on a Hmong girl's aspirations, determining whether she attends classes on a full-time basis after puberty. For many Hmong girls, a tension exists between the sense of traditional cultural identities and the wish to attend school. In part, this tension arises because Hmong girls are considered to be women as soon as they marry, often as young as age thirteen to fifteen years old. They skip adolescence, going from childhood to adulthood with the birth of their first child (Walker, 1991). There is no such thing as adolescence in traditional Hmong culture, especially for girls. There is no concept of self-identity to be developed, there is only the transfer of one's identity to a new family. A girl goes from being a daughter in one clan to being a daughter-in-law in another. The clan identity is safe and protective, but it is also limiting for girls.

In a single generation, Hmong women, like many other women who have come to the United States as refugees, have gone from bamboo huts with dirt floors, where they planned and produced the family food and clothing, buried the placentas of their children, and learned everything by observing other women, to a society in which food production and preparation are no longer a lifetime preoccupation, where they buy ready-made clothing, and where their daughters are required to go to school. Hmong men had considerably more exposure to the industrialized world as soldiers, and as students in the predominantly male schools in Laos.

In Laos, Hmong girls did not go to school, because they had to work and the education of girls was deemed less important than for boys. In the United States, Hmong girls want to be Hmong, marry young, and have many babies; but they also want to be good junior high and high school students, talk on the telephone, go to movies, buy trendy clothes, and chew gum. They take pride in their American friendships, but tend to stay close to their own group because of language and cultural barriers and their enrollment in segregated ESL classes.

Education is altering the Hmong conception of the status and responsibilities of girls, but the changes are very subtle. Of course, some men have always helped their wives, but changes in gender roles were augmented by the interlude of the refugee camps, where sheer boredom from lack of military or farming activities encouraged men to help their wives more. In the United States, some husbands of students help take care of the children, prepare the food, shop, and clean.

Gender Roles Take Precedence

As noted earlier, academic motivation is irrelevant when other cultural priorities take precedence. For Hmong girls, the survival of the

Hmong still means having as many babies as soon as possible. In 1986 it was estimated that the average Hmong woman in the United States had almost nine children (Rumbaut and Weeks, 1986). Motherhood at the age of fourteen and fifteen means an end to academic aspiration, regardless of motivation or achievement. Because the gender role assigned to Hmong girls is not compatible with current educational practices in the United States, a high level of academic motivation is generally irrelevant. Attendance at school by young Hmong girls who are mothers requires tremendous sacrifices or trade-offs on the part of their families to maintain cultural continuity in the home, support successive child births, and accommodate changes in the traditional gender division of labor. Most Hmong are not willing to make these sacrifices or trade-offs, especially when the schools are unwilling to accommodate the demands of motherhood in their junior and senior high schools.

Young Hmong mothers in the United States thus pose an interesting dilemma for educational policy makers. These mothers need an education to help their families become financially self-sufficient, but because there is no room for preschool-age children in most elementary, middle, and high schools, most Hmong mothers must drop out to care for their families. I found that when young mothers drop out, they tend to have more children in rapid succession while they are still of school age. While many Hmong talk about the problems of early marriage, Hmong girls continue to marry young, and since most Hmong women do not use birth control methods either systematically or effectively (Korenbrot, Minkler, and Brindis, 1988), there is no reason to believe that the large number of young Hmong mothers will decline significantly in the near future. Therefore, policy makers are faced with the reality of young, school-age mothers.

There is another conundrum for policy makers. Cumming's (1988) research indicates that Hmong mothers are highly sensitive and responsive, and research on early childhood education has shown the importance of sensitive and responsive mothering in stimulating child development, the connection between early childhood development and future academic success, and the economic advantages of graduating from high school. Yet, as Vang (1992), Vangay (1989), and Walker (1989) have found, most Hmong mothers fail to graduate from high school, many do not make it out of middle school, and almost all are dependent on Aid to Families with Dependent Children. The choice for young Hmong mothers seems to be between continuing to provide good mothering skills to their children by remaining at home (but in so doing, remaining on welfare, dependent and uneducated), and attending school but abandoning their successful methods of mothering because those methods are based on close access to their children and most elementary, middle, and high schools do not allow this. Surely there is a middle ground, but it will cost school districts money to provide extra day care facilities for children. These costs would be justified, however, by the long-run effect of educated Hmong women helping their families get off welfare.

The Value of Good Mothering Skills

Cumming's (1988) research compared Hmong mothers and low-income white mothers in Minnesota. This research reinforced my long-held knowledge that Hmong women are highly skilled mothers and caregivers, and that the reasons are culturally based. Because of my experience of working with Hmong and Mien mothers in the refugee camps of Thailand for three years, I sought out Hmong and Mien women to help me raise my own children. As Cumming found: "The traditional Hmong culture provides the very kind of emotional and physical support, as well as guidance, to mothers that has been found, in studies conducted in the United States, to relate to optimal (i.e., sensitive and responsive) caregiving practices and, ultimately, to secure attachments" (1988, p. 142).

The types of measurements used by Cumming and others in the field of child development are alien to most Hmong mothers, and it would be difficult to explain to uneducated Hmong mothers why these measures are important. It is important, however, for policy makers and educators to recognize that the mothering skills developed in the Hmong culture are consistent with what many child developmental psychologists advocate and what many college-educated mothers aspire to. It is in the best interests of Hmong children's future development, and critical to Hmong women's identity and the economic self-sufficiency of their families, that young Hmong mothers be allowed to practice their traditional skills as mothers without giving up their rights to an education commensurate with their academic potential.

Child psychologists commonly agree that "maternal sensitivity and secure attachments are the patterns consistent with optimal developmental outcome . . . in terms of their relation to children's competence at later developmental tasks (e.g., peer relations, enthusiasm and persistence on task, compliance)" (Cumming 1988, p. 144). Securely attached infants want to be close to their mothers or another primary caregiver, and are easily comforted and reassured when distressed. The mother, or primary caregiver, is the basis of security. The quality of a child's secure attachment is measured by the balance between wanting to be near the mother or primary caregiver and demonstrating confidence to explore the world. Securely attached children have higher overall competence in other domains, including play, self-control, and sociability.

Cumming found that, "without exception, the Hmong refugee children all earned significantly higher Attachment Security scores than the mean obtained by the Caucasian-American children" (1988, p. 136). Maternal sensitivity explained these differences in the level of attachment security and orientation between Hmong and European American groups. All Hmong mothers in Cumming's study scored at the extremely high end of the Ainsworth Maternal Sensitivity-Insensitivity Scale, which means that they were typically rated as "'exquisitely attuned' to the child's signals and [responded] to them promptly and appropriately, without any distortion by her own needs or defenses. When she cannot give the child what he wants, she acknowledges the wish and offers an alternative" (p. 89).

Cumming also found that Hmong mothers scored higher than European American mothers in terms of being "continuously alert to [their children's] whereabouts, activities, and signals and [arranging] the environment and her own activities so that she can readily respond." Furthermore, each Hmong mother in Cumming's study was "highly accepting of her child and his behavior. Although she may, on occasion, be irritated or frustrated by the child's behavior, she expresses respect for his feelings and his value as an individual" (Cumming, 1988, p. 90). Hmong mothers were also found to be "highly cooperative" in that they paced their "interventions so that they did not interrupt" a child's activities, and in that "shifts in activities or interactions [seemed] co-determined" (p. 91).

Cumming found that Hmong mothers' high sensitivity to their children was characteristic at both the newborn and toddler stages. In contrast, half of the European American mothers who were highly sensitive to newborns became insensitive to their children in the toddler stage. The significance of this is that the security attachment of toddlers whose mothers had become insensitive is the same as those whose mothers were also insensitive to them as infants.

The success of the Hmong mother in terms of sensitivity and responsiveness is related to her being accessible to her children, and to the respect her community gives her for this role. Mothering is culturally taught and supported by the Hmong culture. According to Cumming (1988, pp. 141–142), "the Hmong culture, both in Laos and in the United States, embodies a social structure in which child-rearing values and practices have been strictly encoded within an extended family or clan system in which there is a strong priority for attentive and responsive parenting and in which both children and the maternal role are held in high esteem."

This type of finding often leads to the assumption that because Hmong live in family enclaves, there is always a sister-in-law or mother-in-law to take care of the children of young mothers who choose to attend school. This is an incorrect assumption. In-family child care cannot be assumed, because of the high fertility rate among Hmong women of childbearing age. Most sisters-in-law and mothers-in-law have their own young children to care for. It is true, however, that Hmong mothers are supported by their community. Cumming (1988, p. 151) found that, in the Hmong community, "mothers enjoyed almost constant companionship of other women, emotional support, physical assistance, and direct guidance in their roles as mothers."

One does not have to be with Hmong women very long before realizing that motherhood and childbirth are inextricably part of the Hmong cultural identity for women. Although Hmong women are beginning to realize that high levels of fertility limit their educational levels and their opportunities for earning incomes outside the home, motherhood is the Hmong woman's only basis for power in the traditional Hmong culture. The Hmong culture has been held intact partially because of the strong role of mothers. Mainstream American culture pays lip service to the value of motherhood (Lightfoot, 1978) but demands that mothers make a trade-off between being with their children and working, between advancing to high-level positions and part-time work that remains stagnant, between being with their children or getting an education, between participating in politics or any other adult activities and being accessible to their children. The Hmong culture forbids such trade-offs. The ideas of individual independence and self-sufficiency are novel for most Hmong, and the concept of the individual is rarely used in Hmong language. Any valuing of independence or idea of "self" is immediately suspect. In the Hmong culture the family, not the individual, is the unit of labor.

Education threatens Hmong mothers' sensitivity and responsiveness to their children because they are based on the accessibility of the mother. Education also threatens the group support system for Hmong mothers and children by separating the mother from her home. It would seem that it is in the interests of policy planners in the fields of health, education, and welfare to fully understand the role of women in the Hmong culture, and to work together to ensure that the Hmong skills of motherhood are preserved.

The future academic and economic success of the Hmong in the United States would seem to rely in part on perpetuating the Hmong style of mothering; but like other refugee groups before them, the future of the Hmong in United States may also depend on the ability of women to add their income to the family coffers. The vast majority of Hmong women, however, had no formal education before coming to the refugee camps in Thailand, and most Hmong women in the United States remain preliterate in any language. Given this high rate of illiteracy among Hmong women, and given an average of almost nine children per Hmong woman, their need to remain accessible to their children, and the lack of adequate child care facilities in most schools, Hmong mothers will be unlikely to complete their middle and high school education, and therefore will be unable to contribute to the self-sufficiency of Hmong households.

The Small Window of Opportunity

This chapter has tried to show how background and academic motivation play only a secondary role in determining the academic success of groups like the Hmong in U.S. schools. To the extent that teachers recognize how external influences like poverty, war, and American adolescence, and internal cultural influences like assigned gender roles, affect student behavior, the better able they will be to fulfill the needs of a group like the Hmong and help them integrate their old cultural scripts and norms of behavior with their new ones. Understanding the fight for survival will also enable educators to distinguish to some extent those cultural influences that arise in response to conditions in the United States from those that predate a group's arrival in the United States.

The Hmong have lived for a long time with the tension of wanting to preserve their culture while adapting to the modern world, and they have been quite skillful at balancing this tension. As the Hmong become a literate and formally educated people, they run the risk of losing their balance and falling to one of two fates. On the basis of the experiences of previous immigrant groups, it seems that the natural course of events would be for the Hmong cultural identity to break down as they become educated and curious about their new world. Hmong students who do well academically may have to leave behind the group identity. The group identity is so important to the Hmong culture that leaving it behind would be tantamount to leaving behind the Hmong culture. This may be why the grandfather of the shaman at Ban Vinai refugee camp in Thailand predicted that there would be no more Hmong in fifty years.

Alternatively, the Hmong may resist American acculturation. The Hmong fought the Chinese, the Lao, the Vietnamese, and the Thai in order to remain culturally distinct. Past efforts by other immigrant groups to resist acculturation have often been frustrated because new generations are American by birth and do not understand why their grandparents are resisting becoming American. If the Hmong maintain their cultural identity, it may be at the expense of academic and financial success. They might remain a small, poor, minority group.

If the Hmong are wrong in regarding education as their handle on the future, if the majority remain in ESL and low-track, non-college-preparatory classes, and if those who do graduate encounter the "glass ceiling" for minorities in the job market (Ogbu, 1978), the Hmong may join the ranks of other jaded minorities. Hmong youngsters may lose their immigrant vigor and become alienated from school as they realize that they are part of the American underclass. This may already be occurring, as evidenced by the rise of Hmong gangs and generational dependency on welfare. Rather than being regarded as model immigrants, the Hmong and other refugees from Southeast Asia could join Ogbu's category of "involuntary minorities," plagued by a life of alienation and poverty.

The Hmong, like other newcomers and previous immigrants now classified as minorities, have a small window of opportunity. The failure of educators and institutions to recognize their particular cultural strengths, integrate their life experiences into the curriculum, and accommodate the gender roles of Hmong girls will result in a significant setback for the Hmong. One can only hope it will not lead to an expanded body of alienated people, an undesirable outcome by any standard.

5

The Bilingual Education Controversy

I now turn to an analysis of broad problems and solutions related to the education of Asian immigrants and refugees. The case of the Hmong described in the previous chapters will serve as important background in this effort. Although some of the problems faced by the Hmong and by schools in addressing their needs are unique, they also point to broader-based problems affecting all immigrants, including Cambodian, Lao, Mien and Vietnamese refugees, other rural Asian groups, as well as other non-European immigrants. Also, while at the local level teachers and school administrators need to be aware of the specific ethnic backgrounds of their students and the resulting particular cultural impacts on learning, at the policy level broad changes must be made that address a common denominator of success.

Before beginning this analysis, it is important to note that critiques of the quality of education received by newcomers are often stifled out of fear that existing, inadequate programs will be cut further. Such fear should not diminish, however, the need to rethink American goals in relation to the education of all children. In rethinking those goals, educators must learn to respect what newcomers have to say about the education they are receiving, and to use the newcomers' insights to improve American educational systems. For example, students themselves often cry out for a more challenging curriculum. While some school districts may do better than others in teaching Southeast Asians, the programs for new-comer students that I reviewed in Milltown and Rancho Centro are clearly inadequate. It is no wonder—they are based on the idea that there is little we can do. But we can do more.

The Basic Flaw in ESL Programs

A key area of failure in teaching Southeast Asians is in ESL programs. First, the notion of English as a "second" language is a misnomer, since the U.S. education system does not support students in the use of their "first" language. Also, the system labels students who speak another language better than English as "limited," which clearly stigmatizes otherwise potentially talented students and tracks them immediately into low-level courses in which little is expected of them. If the truth be told, it is the *teachers* who often "feel inadequate if you don't speak another language," according to a sixth-grade teacher in Los Angeles who was quoted in the *New York Times* (February 16, 1993, p. C11).

ESL programs have been created to fill the vacuum created by the absence of true bilingual education. Real bilingual education is education in two languages, the child's home language and English. The Lau guidelines that shaped bilingual education in the 1970s determined that ESL classes were not a good enough substitute for bilingual education. Nevertheless, the terms "bilingual" and "ESL" are often used interchangeably; and the original idea becomes even more confused when bilingual education is not available, or when classrooms are multilingual and school districts assume that ESL programs are the next-best thing to bilingual education. In the absence of genuine bilingual education, the second-language concept assumes a derogatory connotation because, as already noted, there is no education in a "first" language.

Furthermore, what Southeast Asian leaders want for their youngsters are classes that teach their children to speak English properly, and not just "as a second language." In other words, these classes should simply be called "English" classes, as some school districts already do. The goal of such programs should be for students to be as strong in English as they are in their home language—essentially, to have two first languages.

To be successful, students need to be able to speak, read, and write English correctly. Proper English classes can introduce the rigor of thought and discipline of application that students will need later to advance in employment skills, to participate in the political process, and for continuing education. Federal, state, and local educational agencies all must recognize that there are no quick or cheap fixes, no miracle methods, and no short-cut strategies to meeting the educational demands of a multicultural student population. Only hard work, perseverance, and commitment on the part of teachers, students, and parents will result in a well-educated generation prepared to bring this country through the twenty-first century.

The Theory of Bilingual Education

Despite persistent criticism, the idea of bilingual education is solidly grounded in results. The problem, as mentioned above, is not with the theory, but that the theory has rarely been applied in practice for students from Southeast Asian backgrounds. The basic idea of bilingual education is that skills developed in a child's stronger language—such as multiplication skills (Hakuta and Snow, 1986) or even linguistic skills (Lanauze and Snow, 1988)—can be more easily transferred to English than skills learned in a language a child does not fully grasp. Also, learning English, or any other language, is usually more successful when a child has a strong foundation in his or her home language (Hakuta, 1986). Perhaps the most persuasive argument for bilingual education, however, is based on studies first conducted more than thirty years ago (Peal and Lambert, 1962). These studies found that students who were able to speak and understand two languages well were better able to formulate concepts and were stronger in tasks that required mental flexibility than monolingual students who came from the same socioeconomic background (Hakuta, 1986; Snow, n.d.a, n.d.b; Cummins, 1976).

Much of the research in the field of bilingual education is actually focused on literacy rather than on linguistics, which is what is implied in the name "bilingual." Much genuinely bilingual education has been conducted in literate (as opposed to oral) languages, such as Spanish, French, Norwegian, and Finnish. In many cases, the research has been focused on reconciling literacy skills in two languages, as in the transfer of such skills as organizing a paragraph or using complex or descriptive sentences. The problem here is that the means of transferring literacy skills from one literate language to another do not apply to students from oral traditions.

Introducing literacy skills to students from oral traditions is an area of research that is relatively undeveloped. In the refugee camps in Thailand, the Consortium, a program funded by the U.S. State Department that prepared refugees for life in the United States, found that Hmong and other preliterate people could better understand what another language was after they had became literate in their home languages. The child's acquisition of literacy skills first in his or her home language also deserves further exploration, because the very skills that are supposed to benefit from bilingualism—concept development and literacy skills in English—are the two areas in which Hmong students have the most difficulty.

Regardless of its promise in theory, bilingual programs have not helped Southeast Asian students in this country for two primary reasons. One is that there are few qualified Hmong or other Southeast Asian teachers; the other is that many refugees and immigrants are not literate in their home language, even if they are otherwise well educated. The first reason is particularly important: the transfer to English of skills developed in a child's stronger language, such as multiplication, is not possible unless there are fully bilingual teachers who can do more than just translate words. Skill development does not occur in isolation. The development of basic skills—

such as math, eye-hand coordination, and time-on-task ability—is embedded in the context of culture. Translated words are not adequate without "translated" cultural context.

A final word needs to be said regarding research on bilingual education. Although such research often focuses on the importance of transferring literacy skills from one language to another, recent studies have indicated that students who are new to English also benefit from early development of literacy skills in English (Walker, 1990; Samway, 1992). In particular, Samway found that "contrary to popular belief, children acquiring English as a second language are capable of successfully communicating their thoughts and experiences in writing without first having attained high levels of oral proficiency in English." Nevertheless, the emphasis in most ESL programs, such as those offered to Southeast Asian students in Milltown and Rancho Centro, is on development of English oral skills to the detriment of English writing skills. This was the single most salient concern that emerged from interviews with students, parents, and teachers in both school districts. This issue will be explored further in the next chapter.

Community Opposition to Bilingual Programs

Available research makes clear that if there are qualified Hmong, Cambodian, Khmu, and Lao teachers in the classroom, "including instruction in their native languages as part of their educational programs will promote and not impede their progress" (Snow, p. 20, n.d.b.); but rather than a true bilingual education, what many Southeast Asian students received in Milltown and Rancho Centro was a watered-down curriculum and simplified English offered in segregated classrooms. None of their classroom teachers were able to understand or speak the students' primary languages, and little concerted effort was made to help Southeast Asian bilingual aides become certified teachers.

As a result, Southeast Asian community leaders were generally opposed to both ESL and bilingual education. It is no wonder that interviews with Hmong leaders revealed confusion about what actually constituted bilingual education and how it differed from ESL programs. Teachers and administrators frequently referred to ESL classes with all or mostly Hmong students, that were taught by monolingual English speakers, as "Hmong bilingual classes."

There are, however, other reasons why the Hmong have opposed bilingual education. One is that they have never truly known it—not in Laos, not in the United States. For the Hmong, going to school has *always* meant studying in another language. In the Laos mountains, those youngsters who were fortunate enough to attend school were immersed in Lao and French. (Perhaps it is no wonder that so few succeeded academically.) In the United States, the majority of Hmong students have been tracked into ESL classes. Chou Tou, a Hmong educated in France who worked with a Hmong community agency, said, "To my memory I have never got the memory that I didn't know the Lao language. For me, the concept of separating language, that's an adult concept. [ESL is OK] for adult school, that's OK, ESL. But for kids, normally you should be able to put them directly into English or mixed classes. Normally they should be able to survive, to swim in a new culture, a new language."

What Chou Tou failed to mention was that because of the small sizes of Hmong villages and the great distances between them, bright Hmong children were usually sent to Lao villages to study, where they were immersed in the Lao culture and language both inside and outside of school. Some gifted boys were then placed in French secondary schools, where they became effectively trilingual. Historically, most Hmong girls were unable to attend any school because their parents feared for their safety. Few girls, therefore, learned Lao, and fewer still learned French—formerly the languages of politics, commerce, and academics in Laos.

In the United States, historically, the immersion method has often alienated entire language communities, resulting in high failure and dropout rates among students from non–English-speaking backgrounds. Recent evidence also shows that, contrary to popular belief, children of earlier immigrants from Europe who were immersed in English at school also had a high failure rate (Perlmann, 1988; Farley and Neidert, 1984). Whether this failure rate resulted from overcrowded classrooms, poverty, cultural differences, language difficulties, or all of the above has not been determined. It would seem, however, that Jewish, Chinese, and Japanese students who came from academically oriented families and were provided after-school programs and Saturday schools to maintain their home cultures and languages fared better. While such supplementary programs were by no means the only reason for the relative academic success of these immigrant groups, it is significant that these three groups were among the most successful in educational achievements. Nevertheless, it must be recognized that, although the few Southeast Asian refugees who have succeeded academically have been immersed in English-only classes, all of them have related how painful this experience was—especially for those placed in classes below their age or ability level. The few success stories must be measured against the psychological pain caused by immersion in the new culture and alienation from one's home culture. It must also be kept in mind that these individuals are exceptional by any standard, and probably would have succeeded in any type of program.

Because of the absence of certified Southeast Asian teachers, ESL types of programs have been perceived as the only alternative to full immersion of Southeast Asian LEP students in mainstream classes. On the positive side, in many cases caring ESL teachers have become advocates for the newcomers, and ESL teachers have often become the only personnel with any understanding of Southeast Asian cultures. On the negative side, however, many ESL teachers have thought they were doing a good job educating Hmong in ESL-type classes, simply because the Hmong earned high grades; and many have believed that it is better for Hmong and other LEP students to be isolated rather than to be immersed in regular classes and expected to compete with native English speakers. Furthermore, ESL is often seen as an easy way out of a tough problem. Teachers have explained they do not have enough time in regular classes to meet the special challenges of students learning English, and they have often regarded communicative ESL methods—that is, instruction based on casual conversation and survival vocabulary—as a breakthrough in the tedium of grammar-based instruction. They have enjoyed using these methods to teach Southeast Asian students, even though the students have not been receiving the level of instruction they truly need.

The harshest critics of ESL have often been those the program was meant to serve—in this case, the Hmong. Hmong leaders are concerned about inferior education in ESL programs. For example, Chou Tou regarded ESL classes as a "trap," because they track children in the lowest levels and do not enable them to compete with other students. In his words: "Personally, I don't like the [ESL]. It's really a trap to trap people to the wrong track. Because in Laos, in order to be able to compete with Lao children or Lao people at the same level, you should speak Lao as well as the Lao. In this country if we keep on talking [ESL], at age four we talk Hmong culture only. How many chances do we have to go to Harvard? No chance."

Chou voiced the high expectations Hmong have for their youngsters: "We should master, we should be able to master the English language . . . as well as any American people." He worried that the low level of tracking would make "fifth-class citizens" out of the Hmong. From the perspective of their leaders, the Hmong have much to learn in order to catch up. Chou argued that the Hmong are "coming from the sixteenth century into the twenty-first century. In this country the first thing we need is technology and know-how, technical, [and] electronic."

A further concern of Southeast Asian leaders in the United States is that Southeast Asian children are missing the content of subject areas. For example, in Milltown, an elementary or middle school ESL teacher was expected to teach math, science, English, and social studies; but the Southeast Asian leaders there said some teachers used all the class time to teach English, and so the children missed the other subjects. They claimed that other teachers raced through all the subjects, and did not really have enough time to teach. According to Joua Kue, Milltown's home liaison, who was introduced in Chapter Three: "The big problem is that it does not matter what method or what materials they teach; one teacher teaches everything, science, math, and English together. They say in one day a teacher can teach three or four things, but the teacher doesn't really teach three or four things. . . . The teacher may teach English, and time passes by and he doesn't have time to teach other [topics]. . . . The teacher doesn't allow time to concentrate on the subjects that the student could really understand."

The result in Milltown was that Milltown teachers did not teach the Hmong children what they needed to know to get into good high schools or to get into good colleges. According to Joua, "I can see, in the future, if we don't change the program, the teaching curriculum now, in the next ten years our kids will be still just the same as the ones who just came from Thailand. The curriculum now, they don't teach the kids to reach the maximum so they can go to good high school, [get] good grades, and [go to a] good college. They only teach them survival and to get through."

Research with other groups supports the concern that ESL classes are teaching simplified English and lower levels of interpretive and comprehensive skills than Hmong and other Southeast Asian students are capable of learning. Luis Moll (1992) and Moll and Diaz (1982) found that English teachers underestimate the learning capabilities of Spanish speakers who are learning English because of the students' problems with English pronunciation. They wrote, "Teachers may take unfamiliarity with English as indicative of decoding problems which leads them to focus on low level skill development rather than on promoting the higher order interpretive skills that students may actually be capable of handling." A bilingual professor at the University of Rhode Island said that most people are of average intelligence, but most ESL programs are geared to the lowest common denominator of intelligence.

Lao, Hmong, and Cambodian leaders all expressed the wish that American schools allow teachers to teach one subject per day. This is how they were taught in Asia under the French system. The Southeast Asian leaders in Milltown were frustrated that there was no similar central standardization of education across the United States.

Communicative/Integrative Approaches

Most of the ESL and other programs for Southeast Asia refugee children rely on the communicative or integrative approach to teaching a foreign language, which is characterized by conversational phrases and object-focused vocabulary, rather than on the traditional approach, which is based on grammar and rote memorization of dialogues. The problem with the communicative approach is that when it is taught in isolation it tends to minimize vocabulary, provide only limited context for new words, and simplify English sentence structures.

Building confidence in English is the key to most ESL programs. There is little or no disagreement among researchers about the importance of confidence. However, in the effort to develop that confidence, English learners have been segregated and taught simplified English. Most students' first priority is social, and they are embarrassed by their babylike English. To supplement what they learn in class, they may focus their attention on developing the street slang common in the low-income areas where most refugee youngsters live. Serious students have to develop their academic skills all over again in order to compete with their peers; and all students need to develop an internalized understanding of English grammar and syntax, and such specialized skills as taking standardized tests and writing nativelike English.

A particular complaint of Hmong and Cambodian community leaders is that teachers of communicative-type programs neglect all-important instruction in English grammar and syntax. A Hmong boy interviewed in St. Paul for the National Coalition of Advocates for Students' 1988 Immigrant Students' Project said he wanted to learn grammar so he could understand English, not just learn to speak. The slow pace of his classes frustrated him. Southeast Asian community leaders tend to prefer the structural or rule-oriented approach, because most of them were educated in their first countries under strict French systems. From their perspective, the communicative or integrative type of instruction in the United States may be adequate for adults, but not for youngsters who aspire to fluency.

It is hardly surprising therefore that Southeast Asian leaders were unanimous in saying that the most important thing for their children to learn at school is English composition and syntax. In Milltown, Sothit Ngor, the Cambodian resource teacher, and guidance counselor Dom DePetri agreed that the ability to write well in English was the *sine qua non* for achievement in the American school system. The Cambodian resource teacher identified two problems that were common concerns of refugee populations everywhere. The first was learning to write well in English; the second was survival. Chou Tou, the Hmong community worker in Rancho Centro who was educated in France, believed in no uncertain terms that "the problem is the language because the problem is we are here. In order to be able to survive in the twenty-first century, the first thing we should know is the English language."

Such concentration on composition and syntax is exactly what is missing from most integrative and communicative ESL strategies. They are predicated on two primary sources of supposed motivation for wanting to learn a second language: an integrative motivation, driven by the desire to communicate and socialize with speakers of another language; and an instrumental motivation, driven by utilitarian concerns such as the use and profitability of speaking that language (Gardener and Lambert, 1972). As a result of these assumptions, most programs for English learners focus primarily on speaking. Such an approach may serve an American businessperson well when he or she is trying to learn another language, but it does not serve immigrant students who are motivated by a number of other reasons, including pride, self-esteem, the desire for power, and the need, in response to complex cultural pressures, to be fluent and fully literate in their new home language.

Whole Language and Sheltered English

Within the context of the communicative approach, two popular strategies, Whole Language and Sheltered English, have been adapted to meet the massive influx of Southeast Asian and other non–English-speaking children in an environment of funding limitations, lack of materials, and lack of certified bilingual teachers. Whole Language is a strategy that aims at bringing good literature into the school curriculum. Sheltered English is, as its name suggests, an approach aimed at sheltering students in classes in which they do not have to compete with regular students.

Whole Language Strategies

The idea behind Whole Language is that children learn reading, writing, speaking, and thinking together from reading good literature, rather than in separate units. Whole Language can be used to acknowledge and draw from students' cultures in the classroom. In Hawaii, a Whole Language approach enabled the Kamehameha Early Learning Project, introduced in Chapter Four, to incorporate the native Hawaiian Creole tradition of telling a story cooperatively into the school curriculum. As a result of allowing students to use their traditional learning skills, verbal I.Q. scores increased (Cummins, 1984).

The Milltown schools have also used Whole Language approaches. Milltown teachers have different ideas about this approach to LEP students. Cambodian resource teacher Sothit Ngor said, "Whole Language, I think it's good, but it depends on the teacher, how well the teacher has adopted the method, or not. And how much they can get the students in the classroom writing well. About the teaching method, it is good for some students to learn to speak, to communicate faster, but I find they have problems with survival." Sothit said that the focus of Whole Language in the classrooms he visited was picture cards with words on them.

Guidance counselor DePetri thought the concept of Whole Language was good, but he wondered if it could also be "very dangerous," because

> it does not explain the rules of English grammar. How do you possibly diagnose a child's problem with Whole Language? When a child asks 'Why does that word have -ed?' 'Oh, you don't have to know that it is a verb and it is past tense and there are certain rules.' That Whole Language drives me up a wall. I have adjusted my classes to use Whole Language concepts, but don't tell me to throw away my grammar books. The kids have to learn how to write. The kids who are most successful are the kids who can write a composition. Bottom line. You're not going to get that in Whole Language. Because especially in ESL, if you don't explain the rule to them, they are going to keep making the same mistake. But the Whole Language concept I think is excellent. The kids are learning a lot more. But don't throw away everything. It's the new way, but it could be very dangerous.

An elementary school teacher in Milltown liked the Whole Language approach without reservation. She said, "I think Whole Language is a much better approach, . . . [a] wholistic approach—using a lot of language experiences and concrete things that their minds can hold on to. Start with a book, try to bring in objects that relate to that story or experiences, then have kids make a book, identify words, symbols. After we make the book, we go back to it all year long."

The Sheltered English Approach

Conversely, Sheltered English is "an instructional approach used to make academic English understandable to LEP students. Students in these classes are 'sheltered' in that they do not compete academically with native English speakers since the class includes only LEP students. . . . In the Sheltered English classroom, teachers use physical activities, visual aids, and the environment to teach important new words for concept development in mathematics, science, history, home economics, and other subjects" (Freeman and Freeman, 1988, p. 1).

There are two salient problems with Sheltered English. The first is that Sheltered English is based on the deficit theory. "Sheltered" means to be protected. It implies that LEP students are deficient and must be protected from competition with other students because they speak another language better than English. This approach is debilitating for all of the students as well as the teachers. Rather than regarding multiple linguistic abilities and multicultural knowledge as an academic asset of the individual students and a source of information for the entire class, it is treated as a handicap.

The second problem with Sheltered English is that every teacher seems to define this strategy differently. In their lengthy study of California schools, McLaughlin, Minicucci, Nelson, and Parrish (1992) could not even define the concept. Instead, they explained that, "in practice, the Sheltered English approach is often used eclectically, and many teachers and administrators could not clearly articulate what the approach means. Many meanings seem to have evolved, and we found that the teachers using the method vary greatly in how strictly they employ the strategies and techniques." It is not even clear if Sheltered English is an ESL method or another distinct strategy.

In 1985, Krashen introduced a model that suggested that Sheltered English was a method for teaching ESL. He proposed that it be used to move students gradually from studying all their core subjects in their first language to being mainstreamed. The idea was that beginning ESL students would be mainstreamed in music, art, and physical education, while they studied ESL separately from mainstream students and studied all of their core subjects in their first language. At the intermediate level, ESL, math, and science would all be taught in a sheltered classroom; and at the advanced level, language arts and social studies would be taught in this milieu. While the theory sounds adequate, the real problem is that there is little or no core-subject instruction in the first language of most Southeast Asian students. As a result, Southeast Asian students are often taught Sheltered English in lieu of core subject material.

There are also problems regarding other assumptions upon which Sheltered English is based. The Sheltered English strategy used in Rancho Centro is based on the outdated theory that language acquisition occurs in lockstep stages, even though "evidence has been accumulating in the past several years that the process of L1 [first language] learning may be less uniform than previously thought" (Wong Fillmore and Valadez, 1987). The assumption is that language acquisition is the same as early childhood development; but this is a patronizing, degrading, and demoralizing attitude for students. There is no research to support the notion that the average LEP student operates with the same level of development as a two-year-old, the characteristic age of many of the stages assumed in this strategy. We know from research in bilingual education that, for all but a few, the skills acquired during these stages have already been developed in the home language. The correct question to ask is how to connect those skills to a new language, not how to reproduce skill development from scratch.

Furthermore, Sheltered English often equals simplified English. One approach taught in many California school districts actually encourages teachers to simplify the English and the content of regular textbooks (Northcutt and Watson, 1986). This strategy deprives Southeast Asian students of the very things they need most: an ear for nativelike English, an understanding of English syntax, an understanding of the correct use of prepositions, and the ability to write an English composition. Students are not easily fooled by the Sheltered English approach. For all intents and purposes, it is baby talk, and is an insult to the students' sense of self.

Despite its problems, the Sheltered English approach is very seductive for school districts that may be required by law to train teachers who are not certified. Sheltered English requires instructors to know no other language than English, and it does not specifically require knowledge and awareness of the students' family backgrounds, of students' particular cultural influences and their effect on learning, or even of students' life histories. If a teacher understood the Hmong culture or general refugee experience well enough, with the help of a bilingual aide, she or he might be able to help link the Hmong history with a new understanding, and at the same time facilitate new insights and perspectives for other students. Sheltered English also tends to serve the teacher's needs rather than those of the student. Like most ESL strategies, Sheltered English is a theory developed by researchers who are out of touch with Southeast Asian students, if not students from other cultures. After a brief period of popularity, Sheltered English has been shown to be based on false simplifications. It tends to ignore who people are and what their needs are.

In defense of the idea, however, Francisca Sanchez of the Alameda County Office of Education in California is one who has attempted to set standards for Sheltered English instruction. Sanchez (1989, p.18) explained, "Sheltered English does address the core curriculum and provides LEP students with a variety of interactive means to accessing that curriculum." Sanchez also stated that "Sheltered English is not 'watered down' instruction, nor 'remedial' instruction. It does not involve a less rigorous nor an alternative curriculum" (p. 1). Sanchez emphasized the importance of respecting the core curriculum and connecting prior knowledge and concept development; but these are common good educational practices and do not require a specialized, Sheltered English approach. They can even be applied to the education of proficient English speakers, as will be discussed in the next chapter, on family-based multicultural education.

Separate But Equal?

The Hmong regard English as their handle on the future. They believe that to survive in this country they must first speak English, and then understand the political system. Hmong community leaders are opposed to bilingual or ESL classes that separate their children from the mainstream because they believe segregation hinders rather than helps them to progress. Many of the classes in the lower elementary grades in certain schools in Rancho Centro were predominantly or entirely Hmong. In other classes, one-half to two-thirds of the students were Hmong. The rest of the students were mostly Hispanic. Only a few students in these classes spoke English as their home language. Chou said he had a file of complaints from Hmong parents, "Some because their children don't speak English. Some because their children are in classes that are only refugee kids. The more serious are those that ask about the classes that put only refugee kids together."

Hmong parents say they would like their children to have extra classes in English before and after school, in addition to the regular curriculum. As shown in Chapter Three, the families of refugee youngsters are willing, even eager, to have their children remain at school longer to ensure that they will get the extra help they need. Instead, according to Chou, Hmong children in Rancho Centro were in segregated classes and received an inferior education. About mainstream classes in schools where almost all of the students are Hmong, he said,

> They learn not enough. For example, my daughter, she goes to [the Horn] School—she's in the first grade. It's probably subjective. To me it seems that she goes too slow. Now the year is almost finished, right? She can't speak English. She is six years old. She was born in France. Last year I put her in kindergarten in [another school district] for just three months. It seems she did much better. After three months she spoke English. Now

after one year she can't speak English. That's inconceivable for me. In her class there are thirty-one kids . . . and probably eight to ten mainstream people. Instead of coming home with English, some days she comes home with Lao language. I was surprised. . . . Normally the young kids could do better in the schools. In some classes there are too many Hmong.

In Milltown, elementary and middle-school students were placed in self-contained ESL classrooms until they tested as fluent in English. They usually remained in these classrooms for two to three years, moving from one level to the next, and were integrated with mainstream students only for gym and lunch. The ESL classes included not just Southeast Asian students, but students of several races who spoke several different languages. At one Milltown elementary school with a large Southeast Asian population, there were ten to fifteen Hmong in an ESL class, along with Spanish-speaking students, speakers of other languages, and some English speakers. One teacher claimed that the monolingual English-speaking students placed in the ESL classes were actually African American students and "slow" students who were placed there to fill out the quota of twenty-eight students per class that was agreed to in the teachers' contracts.

Hmong leaders in Milltown were particularly disturbed by the self-contained classrooms. They argued that these settings did not prepare Hmong students for the mainstream. In 1987, Joua Kue, the home liaison, said,

I have been working with the school department of Milltown for eight years, and they have changed this method for only three years. The child who came before that had the chance to go to ESL for one or two hours and to go to regular classes, but now they changed to the self-contained classroom. I can see that in the future the child who is in the middle school and elementary school, they cannot go far. They will end up with high school and drop out, and that is worth nothing. They cannot compete; they cannot take high school English and high school history.

In Milltown, a typical high-school-age student who was not proficient in English had three hours a day of ESL; an intermediate ESL student had two hours a day; and an advanced ESL student had one hour a day of ESL. The beginning ESL student filled the rest of his or her schedule with electives like shop, typing, or cooking. The intermediate and advanced ESL students could select transitional science, history, math, social studies, or ESL reading by computer. In some other California schools, newcomers spent four periods a day in ESL, and were integrated in gym only. This is a lot of hours to spend in ESL classes when many ESL teachers have not been trained to teach these students.

It is important to include here the findings of research on bilingual education reported by Wong Fillmore and Valadez (1987) that validated the concern of Hmong leaders about segregated classes. These studies found that classes that have equal numbers of primary English speakers and English-learning students are ideal to promote interaction. Wong Fillmore and Valadez argued, "In order to learn the target language, there must be opportunities for the learners and speakers to come into contact and reason for them to communicate in a cooperative fashion" (p. 40). Even if the method of instruction is communicative or integrative, it does little good if Hmong students are only communicating and integrating with other students who are learning English.

Joua Kue said, "For a child to be able to compete with American children, you have to learn the way of American kids, give them a chance to integrate with all American groups. So if they do not learn from the teacher, they can learn from their American friends. Some ESL is good, but not all day and all year." An elementary principal in Rancho Centro agreed with him: "Let's face it," she said, "they learn more English from the other boys and girls than they do from us, and if they are only speaking with other Hmong children, they are not going to be using English. More has to be done with American children and ESL and Asian population, assimilating them more together."

There is, of course, a difference between playground English and classroom English. A child may speak English without an accent and sound fluent when he or she is playing with his or her friends, but it does not mean that the child also understands academic English equally well. Student abilities in English will also differ by the content area, reflecting the student's background in that area. It is commonly understood that written English is different than spoken English.

The English of testing also differs from spoken English, but unfortunately standardized tests are the commonly used means for placing Hmong and other English-learning students in grades and levels of classes. Such tests are also used to measure their proficiency level in subject areas. Hmong students are consistently tracked in the lowest levels right from the beginning, because they systematically score low on standardized placement tests. Sothip Ngor, the Cambodian resource teacher in Milltown, was disturbed that all Cambodian children were automatically placed in easy classes, regardless of their intelligence. He said, "I am bringing some Cambodians to them, and they just put them in the class for woodworking and art and math and ESL. I can see some of them need it, but others transferred from upper classes [in other states]. They should get something better for [those] kid[s]." Ironically, these tests have often been administered to Southeast Asian students by Southeast Asians hired by school districts because of their intelligence, ability, and understanding of Southeast Asian cultures. Yet such employees were never allowed to use their discretion to determine the level or class for which each child was best suited; they were only allowed to give the tests, which contain no such sensitivity. The use of such subjective measures as discretion was usually left to the teacher, who often did not have the insights of the Southeast Asian teachers' aides.

It should be noted that the average Hmong scores have improved in recent years, but still remain low when compared to the Vietnamese, for example. One reason for this change is that Hmong students have become more familiar with taking such tests. However, as noted in Chapter Four, standardized tests require skills that are not developed by the traditional Hmong culture that emphasizes cooperative learning and oral information. Most Hmong students still lack decontextualizing skills in reading, word recognition skills, and expository writing skills because reading is not part of the home culture.

It is now commonly accepted that standardized tests cannot test learning aptitude across cultures. For example, Hmong culture does not include the Aristotelian types of definitions assumed on many U.S. standardized tests. Snow (p. 11, n.d.b.) found in a study at the United Nations International School "that children's abilities to give formal definitions related strongly to their scores on the language and reading subtests of the California Achievement Tests." This correlation illuminates why word recognition and expository writing are two areas in which Hmong had the most difficulty.

Despite the proven impact of such cultural factors, the use of standardized tests is pervasive. Milltown, like many other school districts around the country, used the IDEA Proficiency Test in kindergarten through eighth grade, and the Modern American English Proficiency test in high school, to place students in classes. Hmong students in California had to receive a score on a placement test at or above a certain level in order to enter mainstream classes. This level was determined by the individual school sites or by the district. Even if a student wanted to move into a higher-level class because his or her other work was too easy, he or she could not do so unless he or she received an adequate score. All elementary students in Rancho Centro thus had to take a district proficiency test to graduate from the eighth grade and go to high school. One of the Title VII teachers estimated that "the Hmong and Hispanics, the minority students, were about 50 percent on grade level even in seventh and eighth grade, but their rate of passing that proficiency test was only 40 percent compared to the overall passing rate of 80 percent."

A National Challenge

It is important to remember that the job of providing an equal educational opportunity to newcomers—and to Hmong in particular—is difficult, and will be costly in the short run. In the long run, however, the costs of good education are far less than the costs of lifelong or generational welfare dependency, social alienation, and bitterness.

As mentioned in Chapter Three, the cost of educating Hmong and other immigrant students is a legacy of federal immigration policies. Most state-based ESL and other programs for those who are learning English pay lip service to the commendable ideals of federal bilingual laws and the bilingual movement, but they are not bilingual programs. States simply cannot afford to hold local school districts to standards for bilingual students established on the national level. The result is a cat-and-mouse game involving ideal guidelines with no adequate means of meeting them. Sufficient funding is the minimal requirement for ensuring, for one thing, that school districts can provide career ladders for classroom aides to become bilingual teachers in Southeast Asian languages.

But the real issue is deeper: Can we face up to who we are as a nation and address the needs of students who require considerably greater attention than they are now receiving? This will require national resources and additional commitment by teachers to not reach out so much for a new "program" or "strategy." It will require instead that all of us reach out to other cultures and learn from the students themselves and their families.

∽∽ 6
The Promise of Family-Based
Multicultural Education

In the last chapter I focused on problems that currently prevail with ESL practices. I now suggest ways to improve the education of Hmong and other Southeast Asian students, as well as other non-European immigrant or refugee students, using strategies developed from a family-based multicultural educational theory. Family-based multicultural education can replace the deficit theory illustrated in prior chapters, which has resulted in the teaching of English as a "second" language even though no first language is taught, and the labeling of English-learning students as "limited." The goal of family-based multicultural education is to connect home cultural knowledge and school learning. It is based on the hope that educators might focus on what children already know and use it as a foundation to build on, add to, and connect with new knowledge. If educators focus only on what the child does not know, the risk is great that the child will feel denigrated and insulted and ultimately become alienated by the education system.

Family-based multicultural education can be the first step on a long road to recognizing that diversity is a strength in the U.S. education system, not a weakness. Family-based multicultural education

---

Portions of this chapter previously appeared in Cabello, JoAnn (ed.), *California Perspectives: An Anthology from the Immigrant Students Project*, winter 1990, 1, pp. 17–21.

requires truly multicultural classrooms, not segregated ones where Hmong and other English learners are taught separately. Furthermore, family-based multicultural education is not intended to substitute for the development of core English classes. Developing family-based multicultural education to its full potential will also require ongoing teacher workshops that allow teachers time to connect its fundamental ideas with their prior professional knowledge.

Family-based multicultural education does not in any way supplant the need for bilingual teachers in Hmong and other Southeast Asian languages. The latter part of this chapter discusses programs for beginning to utilize cultural liaisons in the schools in the form of bicultural and bilingual counselors to work with students, teachers, and parents.

The Strength of a Multiculture

The biggest challenge facing new Asian Americans and their children in U.S. public schools is the diversity of the Asian people. Teachers with limited experience of Asian American cultures may tend to rely on stereotypes of all Asians that ignore the cultural differences among the various groups. Southeast Asian students may be perceived, for instance, as good students who do not need special attention; as English-learning children with limited academic potential; or as gang members. Even those educators who do have an appreciation for cultural diversity may take another dangerous approach. They may limit cultural difference to a discrete number of individual cultures that somehow go together to make up a "multiculture." Such a compartmentalized approach, I believe, may hinder the design of an effective multicultural learning program as much as the approach that ignores cultural differences. There are four main reasons. First, culture cannot be simplified to a static, nondynamic model, especially in as fluid a milieu as the United States. (In fact, as the long-term history of the Hmong demonstrates, flexibility is essential to the survival of a culture.) Second, there is no possible way to enumerate the number of cultures in the

United States, especially when the cultural differences within individual cultures can be as extreme as those between cultures; thus it is impossible for most teachers to understand fully all of the cultural variations in their classrooms. Third, such an "enumerative" approach inevitably leads to racial stereotyping, no matter how sensitive the individual, because it simplifies and thereby trivializes culture. Fourth, students often identify with more than one culture.

It is more productive, I believe, to begin by thinking of the United States itself as a multiculture and then to design a program that not so much aims at accommodating all of its separate parts but instead seeks to elicit from students themselves their expressions of their own cultural identities within a broad context. In this way, culture can be used as an exciting resource for learning, rather than being seen merely as a series of obstacles that must be overcome to perpetuate old ways of doing things.

The initial wide disbursement of Southeast Asian refugee students across the United States in the late 1970s and early 1980s provided a fresh start for multicultural education in this country. Teachers who had distanced themselves from multicultural education in the 1960s and 1970s (often because of its racial and political overtones) wanted in the 1980s to learn more about their refugee students. Now, in the 1990s, the diversity of most inner-city classrooms and the increasing diversity of rural and suburban classrooms have forced multicultural education fully into the foreground for all educators.

Stages of Implementation

The proper implementation of a multicultural education strategy involves three phases. I have chosen to call these the descriptive, inquiry, and integrative phases.

The first implementation phase is called *descriptive* because it involves a school district's first attempts to understand the broad cultural background of its students. For example, during the early phase of Southeast Asian refugee resettlement in the United States (1975 to 1981), many teachers, guidance counselors, and administrators encountered Southeast Asian youngsters for the first time. The initial response of many school districts was to provide a few in-service workshops to teachers to introduce them to the cultures of Vietnam, Laos, and Cambodia. Much of this training, however, was broadly descriptive and tended to emphasize the exotic or unusual aspects of these cultures. For example, lists of cultural behaviors were sometimes distributed that included warnings against such actions as touching a Buddhist child's head (because Buddhists believe that the head is sacred); but singling out such issues clouded the fact that many Southeast Asian students are Catholic, Protestant, Animist, Muslim, or Hindu. A serious problem was that consultants hired to provide these workshops often knew a lot about one Asian culture, but little about others. The limited knowledge of consultants about the complex differences between new Asian Americans sometimes combined with the lack of knowledge of the teaching staff to cause the stereotypes about certain refugee youngsters to be accepted as cultural norms of behavior for all Asian American students.

Inquiry is the second stage in the implementation of multicultural education. This stage emerges when a school district seeks information about its students that goes beyond stereotypes and generalities. Rather than seeking to understand specific cultural attributes, educators may participate in in-service workshops that focus on what culture is, what the cultural priorities of a particular group of people are, and how these may influence students' behavior in the classroom. It is at this stage that teachers begin to recognize the importance and wealth of cultural diversity within the various new Asian American groups.

The third phase of multicultural education, which I have called the *integrative* phase, occurs when teachers recognize the value of the diversity among their students, understand that there is no way that they can learn fully about the culture of each student without the student's help, and become open themselves to learning from the students. It is at this point that a home–school connection begins to emerge. This means that students can finally integrate home knowledge with academic learning in all areas of the curriculum. Moll (1992) refers to such a potential as the tapping of home "funds-of-knowledge: the essential cultural practices and bodies of knowledge and information that households use to survive, to get ahead, or to thrive."

Family-Based Multicultural Guidelines

Teachers should be provided with guidelines that allow them to create opportunities to learn from their students. Such guidelines would open new avenues for all cultures and allow for a broad sharing of experiences in a classroom setting. The goal of multicultural guidelines should not be to provide specific new multicultural input, but to show how existing course content can be related to students' lives. It is more important to rouse the curiosity of students, to give them confidence to explore how their world works, to stimulate their critical and creative thinking, and to provide them with analytical tools than it is to give them new facts—even if they are multicultural facts. In science, for example, a multicultural strategy should show not only how Western scientific methods work, but how other cultures have arrived at similar conclusions using other approaches. Multicultural themes may be used to move inquiry a step further, but the primary objective of the guidelines, such as those that follow, should be to overcome the lack of dialogue between immigrants' homes and their childrens' classrooms.

Regard students as a source of information. Teachers should learn from their students, and they should stress the importance of learning about students' cultural priorities, understanding cultural influences on learning behavior, and tapping existing knowledge and diverse backgrounds.

Encourage behavior and discussion that brings the home background of all students into the classroom and enables students new to English to share their knowledge and experiences with mainstream students.

Identify the strengths of children's home cultures. It is useful to think in terms of home background. What experiences and cultural influences does each child bring into the classroom? What are the strengths and weaknesses of those influences?

Respect the knowledge of students' families. A student from a poor, rural, preliterate family can contribute his or her own family's knowledge about traditional water systems, tigers, centipedes, seasonal weather, monsoons, farming, war technology, diseases and other matters. Pictures and films can begin to reveal the depth of specific knowledge that students bring into the classroom.

Avoid assumptions. Within groups there are tremendous class and background differences that influence the skill development, knowledge, and home support for that child. Avoid assumptions about individuals based solely on cultures. Remember, no student living in the United States is purely Hmong, Mexican, Samoan, or Jamaican. They are Hmong Americans, Mexican Americans, Samoan Americans and Jamaican Americans. Even if a student has been born here to a family that has been here for centuries, he or she may still be in any one of various stages of reaction to the dominant American culture. This may cause a tension between the home and the dominant culture. That tension can be resolved by identifying the strengths that both cultures bring to the classroom.

Avoid stereotypes. To present a picture of a typical student from a certain background and to describe cultural characteristics that distinguish that person from other ethnic groups is dangerous because it borders on stereotyping. It could prove embarrassing, particularly in the long run, because cultures are not static.

Avoid tokenism that trivializes culture. Avoid the approach that features such attitudes as "Now we'll talk about African American scientists" or the contributions made by immigrants. Integrate this information throughout the program. Ideally, the contributions of European descendants should be noted the same as all others and treated as only one source of knowledge.

Recognize historical contributions of a culture as one important component in building a student's self-esteem in the classroom.

Avoid "cookbook" strategies that suggest that by adding a few references or changing terminology a standard program will turn into a multicultural one.

Use a sequential strategy that connects students' home experiences with the classroom topic.

Identify and connect existing skills and knowledge in the home language to English without reproducing skill development.

Raise interpretive skills and comprehension levels by specifically teaching what concepts are; do not assume all cultures share the same concepts; and do not simplify concepts.

Emphasize proper English literacy skills, not just oral skills or simplified English.

Use neither language that is value-laden nor language that assumes prior knowledge, nor simplified English.

Develop standardized test-taking skills, including familiarity with the special syntax and vocabulary used on such tests.

Discuss the cultural and gender imbalance of workers in the academic fields and of the various positions in those fields. What were the socioeconomic circumstances that resulted in this imbalance? What barriers prevented women from making more contributions to science, for example? Who has overcome these barriers and how? Are there still barriers for different ethnic groups and for women in any academic or professional areas of study?

Center activities on commonalities and encourage teachers to explore differences from the base of what cultures have in common. For example, the six major themes of the California Science Framework (energy, evolution, patterns of change, scale and structure, stability and systems, and interactions) are common to all cultures, but their uses and development are distinguished by the economic, social, and cultural framework in which people have lived.

Separate and identify myths, legends, beliefs, and values. Values and beliefs are often based on religion, myths, legends, experience, history, and fear. It is important for a student to distinguish among these.

Connect topics with other content areas. Just as it is essential to learn to hook new knowledge to existing knowledge, it is also important to connect what a student is learning in one subject area with what is being taught in others. This is basic to the framework, for instance, of Montessori schools.

Use real role models. Role models may be the single most important component in learning. Students need to meet people who have made contributions to knowledge in big and small ways. In the absence of such people, use photographs and biographies of living people, not cartoon or fictional characters. When introducing historical subjects, ground them by connecting with information about a real person who faced some of the same problems that students face today but in a different time in history.

Home–School Connections

Creating the home–school connection is at the core of family-based multicultural education. The home–school connection begins when students are able to hook into the content of their lessons and connect their past, personal, and family experiences to what is being taught. This connection serves to validate students' own realities and thereby contribute to building their self-esteem, particularly in regard to the content area that spawned the connection.

The process of home–school connection may be said to begin when a teacher can identify each child's individual experience with a subject. Of course, differences in the relevance of content for individual students reflect differences in their home backgrounds and life experiences. Teachers should not assume relevance in any area for any particular student or group based purely on broad notions of ethnicity. For example, the experience of the son of an ethnic Chinese merchant from Saigon will differ markedly from that of an ethnic Vietnamese girl whose parents were rice farmers, even though they both were born in Vietnam. Teachers may, however, find that differences will break down according to rural-urban backgrounds, family educational levels, class, and gender.

Once the teacher begins to understand the background of individual students, he or she will begin to notice other areas of influence. For example, in most nonindustrialized countries, formal science is a subject of interest primarily to the educated and those who live in urban environments. It should therefore come as no surprise that students' whose parents are from rural backgrounds have little prior knowledge or experience with the concept of science as an aspect of formal education. Nevertheless, the lives of their parents as farmers, fishermen, and refugees from war may have provided them with a wealth of primary knowledge about how science operates in the real world. It is up to the teacher to tap these resources and integrate them into classroom discussion and activities. For example, if a teacher makes an analogy to waves in the ocean while studying sound waves, this analogy may be lost on a child who has never spent time at the ocean, whose parents have no knowledge about oceans, and whose culture contains little information about oceans. In this case, the teacher must first show students what a wave is.

Most Hmong, for example, had never seen a body of water larger than a river before coming to the United States, and they did not understand that they crossed the Pacific Ocean when they came to this country. No one bothered to explain to them that they were over water while in the airplane. The result is that we have high school graduates who do not know what the ocean is. Looking out from Stinson Beach in northern California, a bright young Mien woman who had recently graduated from a high school in an urban port community asked me if there was a bridge that connected California with Hawaii. A Hmong youngster in the seventh grade was surprised to find out that the ocean was salty. In contrast, children who are descendants of Vietnamese fishing families or from the coastal area of a Philippine island have a wealth of knowledge about the ocean.

The challenge to teachers is to connect positively with such cultural differences. One strategy teachers may employ is sequential learning: he or she might begin with prior knowledge, such as myths and oral tales about a subject, and then move on to hands-on, experiential demonstrations. Once such a connection has been made, the teacher may introduce new, related subject material in a more conventional manner.

Home–school connection strategies are also a way to empower parents in the education of their children. Regardless of their educational background, parents will want to participate in the education of their children. This is especially true in many Southeast Asian homes, in which education is a family affair. Either the entire family works on a homework problem or no one does. Yet today the reality is that there is little dialogue between Southeast Asian parents and their children's teachers.

Cultural Journalism

In my research of classroom strategies for the Ford Foundation and the National Coalition of Advocates for Students, one of the most effective multicultural strategies I have found for encouraging cross-cultural understanding and cooperation and for decreasing tensions is the use of writing. Strategies that involve writing work as well for mainstream students as they do for students who are learning English, but in my experience they work particularly well in multicultural classrooms that include students from homes where languages other than English are spoken.

Many teachers have begun to use writing to open up a two-way street of cultural communication between themselves and the multicultural classrooms in which they teach. They realize that all children bring their unique cultural scripts into the classroom. More and more teachers are using family stories and autobiographies to learn about their students—who they are, where their families came from and why, and what they believe in. The content of refugee and immigrant lives is vastly different than that of most teachers and some students. Joint recognition of the facts of students' lives and cultures may serve as a foundation for a dialogue. It may also allow the teacher to incorporate the students' backgrounds into the curriculum and thereby use the information as a "hook" for new knowledge in such subject areas as language arts, social studies, science, history, math, and art.

One of the primary problems that both publishers of textbooks and teachers encounter is the idea of creating a curriculum that is relevant to the lives of students from such diverse backgrounds. Yet, as discussed in the section on home–school connections, interest in a subject and the relevance of learning it is key to getting the attention of students, and one effective way of doing this is to attach new knowledge to personal experience. The idea is to get students to talk, write, or draw about themselves, then slowly move to less familiar areas, developing their knowledge and skills in the process. The goal of this approach is to excite students about learning by breaking down the barriers of the unfamiliar and giving them confidence in their abilities.

Cross-cultural journalism is an effective home–school connection strategy. It generates cross-cultural learning by requiring the teacher to identify opportunities for students to introduce their prior knowledge of a subject. Teachers should be cautioned that students will often not do this on their own. For example, for most students the American Revolution and the arms technology of that time are irrelevant to their lives. However, many of the students' relatives, and a few students, have fought in wars; some of them even made their own guns and had to stand close to their enemy to be effective, like the British and American rebels did during the American Revolution. Others have seen or used modern guns. It is necessary for the teacher to draw students out on points that connect home knowledge about such subject areas. The points of connection in this case are guns, war, and gunpowder.

Cultural journalism goes beyond autobiographies and journals in that it incorporates history and events that have shaped students' lives. It recognizes the value of the history, beliefs, and folk wisdom that are passed down through generations in song, poetry, and oral traditions. This knowledge may be known by the students as a family story or as a story told by the community elders. The strategy of cultural journalism involves writing but also goes beyond it. It involves learning by doing. It means learning how something was done before in order to help students to understand why things are now done the way they are. It can also be used to contemplate how those things can be done better in the future. Cultural journalism requires that the teacher become the student and the student become the teacher.

Cultural journalism is a "hands-on" approach to developing home–school connections. Cultural journalism involves having the students interview members of their family or community about a particular issue that is relevant to a topic being discussed in school, and then sharing the results with other students through their writing.

"The idea of having students write about themselves isn't novel," explained Courtney Sweet, a teacher of LEP students in northern California. Sweet is widely recognized as one of the best teachers of cultural journalism in the San Francisco Bay Area. Student writing is a "window into their lives," Sweet says. "How much of a window [students] want to open up is up to them." The job of a teacher is "to make them feel comfortable" opening up—at least that is how Sweet perceives her job. One way she accomplishes this is to explain to her students that "they're part of history—all of us are. What they have to say is important, and we can all learn from others and their experiences."

Sweet came to the writing strategy in what she calls a "birth by fire." She was a new teacher working in Oakland, California, in 1977. Like most teachers, she was not prepared for the diversity among students' cultures she encountered, except for "little bulletins" put out by the school department. The students' writing, she found, definitely helped her to understand her students from Southeast Asia, Mexico, Central America, Hong Kong, and other places. She remembers thinking, "I could get a lot more out of them if I could develop their writing skills." She was surprised with the results. She soon found she became both teacher and student in their classroom.

Adapting new strategies to a classroom is never easy. At first, Sweet found that most of her LEP students did not believe in their ability to write. When they appeared overwhelmed with the task of writing about themselves, she broke assignments "into bite-sized pieces." As a guide she uses *Our Lives*, a book produced by Myron Berkman and his class at Newcomer High School in San Francisco. Sweet has her students read this book and stories written by earlier classes before they write themselves. This, she says, validates their own life experiences. Furthermore, "the students feel safe because someone else took the risk."

The key learning tools are as much grammar as trust. Both are important to bridge the students' confidence in their stories and their ability levels in writing. It is essential that the final product be presented to or shared with an audience in order to provide a goal, as well as a sense of completion and accomplishment. Another key element is setting high standards. "Raise expectations," she says, "and the kids seem to rise to the occasion." By and large, Sweet was amazed by the amount of unsolicited writing her students brought in. She credits the high motivation of her students to showing them what upper-level classes were producing. In turn, they wanted to create something just as good.

One example of unsolicited writing was a life story written by a Cambodian girl. She was not in Sweet's advanced ESL class that had been asked to write about themselves, but she heard about it and asked Sweet if she could participate. This junior high school girl had only been in the country for a year and a half. Sweet recalled her as being very shy: "She was a good student, but she hid a lot. She had a lot to hide." Sweet was surprised when she read her story. According to Sweet, suddenly she "was like a sprinkler, you couldn't turn her off." She has since graduated from a private women's college, a graduate school where she studied international economics, and is continuing to study in Europe. The student wrote,

> I'm having a new life in this country, but I can't forget my past. I've tried to forget it, but I still can't forget. Sometime I dream that my father is teaching me French like he used to do when he was alive, but when I wake up, I know I am mistaken. I hang my head and cry. I can't study or do anything. Nothing can help me to be happy, so I could say that I am a troubled person. I am proud when I come to school or go somewhere else. I don't want to stay home and think a lot about my past. Sometimes my good grades help me to put all the bad things out of my mind. When I get a good grade, I forget everything that makes me feel foolish. After the war, I lost most of my kin. I'll be unhappy as long as I'm alive. Someone who's an orphan like me can't be happy. In the course of my life, I've seen a lot of strange things and a lot of troubles. I've had a lot of experience with starva-

tion and death. I hate war. I want to avoid war. I don't want to see it again. The war orphaned me. [Walker, 1990, p. 18]

Teachers like to think that practicing cultural writing in the classroom empowers students like this young Cambodian girl, because writing validates such students' reality and turns traumatizing experiences into powerful tools that will strengthen them later in life. In the process, such writing also empowers newcomer parents and community leaders, because it forces the younger members of immigrant communities to turn to them for information. The students realize that their parents or guardians may be illiterate and that they represent the very traditions the students are trying to break away from, but that their lives and experiences are still a valuable repository of identity and hope.

In her classes, Sweet also learned that part of the frustration for students, the part that kept them from telling their stories, was not wanting to make public certain experiences that were too painful or too private to share. Part of the problem for students learning English was not knowing how to say certain things. Sweet perceived her job as finding the fine line between privacy and sharing. Sometimes she succeeded, but she worried that some of the quieter students in her class did not get the attention they needed. She explained: "It's hard in a class where every desk is taken. It's a lot easier to give your attention to someone who asks for [it] and reaches out. It's harder to get at the ones who give appearance of not wanting to."

Another teacher in San Francisco developed peer journals to tap student writing. Peer journals are notebooks shared by two students in different subject areas. Their purpose is to bring the content of one area into the other, and vice-versa. For example, a science class might share peer journals with a social studies class. The students could share their knowledge about a particular time in terms of scientific discoveries, technological development, and the economic, political, and social circumstances that were the context in which those developments took place. This teacher often uses peer journalism to bring content into ESL classes and English language mastery into subject areas.

Two fundamental problems that teachers encounter when they attempt to implement cultural journalism in their classroom are overcrowding and teacher burnout. An administrator in the Compton Unified School District, south of Los Angeles, explained that the amount of time teachers can use for writing in the classroom, or for producing student publications, is limited by overcrowding and a lack of interaction with individual students. A teacher is not going to overburden himself by reading thirty-plus papers for each subject every day.

Butler and Thompson (1990) reviewed cultural journalism magazines produced by high school students across the country and found that most had been discontinued. "Problems with funding and school structure, [space] constraints, legal liability, time requirements, commitment and parental perceptions of good practice that demanded certain types of instructions were all acknowledged as reasons for the many defunct projects." Most magazine strategies did not last, because of loss of energy and lack of commitment on the part of students and teachers alike. Those that lasted longest were those that allowed students to do the most work, including the most difficult tasks.

Small sums of money awarded by the San Francisco Education Fund and others eased the process in San Francisco schools. Elliot Wigginton (1986, p. 86), who created the well-known cultural journalism magazine called *Foxfire*, argued that money is not an impediment to good projects. "I had become fascinated, through activities like the newspaper, by how much could be accomplished for a very tiny bit of cash when that cash was multiplied by lots of heads and hands. It still fascinates me, and I've become convinced that one of the greatest adult cop-outs in any school, and the world outside, is the statement, 'We might as well not even try to do that because we don't have the money.'"

Cultural journalism has implications for textbooks. The History and Social Sciences Curriculum Framework adopted in 1987 by the California State Board of Education simply stated that "materials that ignore the importance of cultural diversity in United States history or world history are unacceptable" (History–Social Science Curriculum Framework and Criteria Committee, 1988, p. 3). These demands were regarded as so radically different from what existed that few publishers submitted textbooks to the state with the largest and most lucrative textbook market in the country. The framework stated: "We want students to see the connection between ideas and behavior. . . . We want our students to understand how people in other times and places have grappled with fundamental questions of truth, justice and personal responsibility and to ponder how we deal with the same issues today" (p. 3).

To a large extent, what the framework called for can come from students. The Cambodian girl's story is a testimony of a child's awareness of the connection between ideas and behavior. It provides a sense of how a refugee youngster dealt with truth, justice, and how to accept personal responsibilities in a world turned inside out. It is but one example of what can be learned from students. According to John Kromkowski of the National Center for Urban Ethnic Affairs (*Worldwinds*, 1982), "If American education is going to begin to prepare students and adults to live together in our ethnically, racially, and culturally diverse society, then the curriculum of our schools must reflect that diversity. Students must be provided with opportunities to perceive their own heritage as legitimate. They must get in touch with their own stories and experiences."

Paraprofessionals Connect Homes and Schools

Having outlined a theoretical framework for change in newcomer education, I now present a model program that addresses the need for bicultural and bilingual counselors in elementary and secondary schools. Model programs are important not as blueprints, but because they demonstrate what can be done when a need has been identified and a community has the determination to garner the resources and support necessary to respond adequately to that need. The importance of the particular model I will discuss in the next section is that it operated within the scope and financial limitations of the school and community. Unlike other strategies, it developed broad support among the Hmong, Cambodian, and Lao communities, in the school district, with the teachers' union, and with local and national foundations.

The Milltown Model Program

I witnessed the beginning of a model program for bicultural and bilingual counselors in Milltown. What made this program special was that it resulted from the concern of Southeast Asian leaders that the lack of bicultural counselors was the major impediment to Southeast Asian students' success at school and in getting into college. These leaders believed that the only way for students to advance themselves was to get out of "self-contained" ESL classes and into the college track. They also wanted to initiate a two-way exchange between refugees and the schools. The Milltown model program has the potential to be considered by, and adapted to, the needs of other school districts around the United States with Southeast Asian and other students from families learning English.

The need for Southeast Asian bilingual counselors was one of the key issues that emerged in an education workshop during the Southeast Asian Conference in April 1986, which took place in the state in which Milltown is located. A major impediment for the Southeast Asians in Milltown was that in their state a counselor must be a credentialed teacher with teaching experience, but there were no certified Southeast Asian teachers. Other impediments in Milltown were lack of money and the opposition of the teacher's union to bilingual counselors.

In the late 1980s, Milltown had certified counselors who were bilingual in Spanish and Portuguese. Then a counselor was fired and complained to his union. An arbitrator was brought in and the union won the arbitration settlement. The state's department of education decided that there would be no certification for a counselor with a "bilingual endorsement." In other words, there could be no such thing as a bilingual counselor. Since then, the department of education has refused to view a bilingual counselor as an area of certification.

The Hmong-Lao Unity Association submitted a request for Southeast Asian counselors to the state's education commissioner and superintendent of the Milltown Schools in 1986. The school department insisted it did not have the budget to pay the salaries of Southeast Asian counselors. The department of education refused to consider their request until the Southeast Asians had candidates who met the degree requirements demanded by union agreements and school policies.

In 1987 the Cambodian, Lao, Hmong, and Vietnamese communities in Milltown decided to seek private funding to pay for three paraprofessional counselors or counselor aides. Together a national foundation and the local community foundation funded half the budget that the Southeast Asians asked for in 1987–88, and again in 1988–89. The department of education designated a small sum in 1988–89. Their plan was to ask the state and the district to pay for the paraprofessionals after they had worked in the schools for three years and proved to be effective. The original proposal envisioned three Southeast Asian counselors who would "improve the relations between parents, teachers and children, provide counseling for individual parents and children so children [could] quickly enter the mainstream and also to help with the proper choice of courses with a view to possible higher education, and provide leadership workshops, particularly in education for Southeast Asian students in middle and high schools."

The Southeast Asians asked permission of the school department to allow three counselor aides to work with the Southeast Asian students and their parents. The Southeast Asians assumed they would be allowed to "work with the principal of each school and consequently have ready access to the teachers and students." The Milltown school department recognized the need for Southeast Asians counselors, but insisted on calling them "paraprofessional counselors" rather than "counselors," for obvious political reasons.

The Hmong, the Lao, and the Cambodians each hired one individual. Tai, the Hmong man, was a graduate of the state university. Davy, the Cambodian woman, was the mother of five children, and was studying to become a nurse. Bounmy, the Lao man, was fairly well educated and very articulate.

Bounmy described the jobs of paraprofessionals during their first year as "trying to get parents to understand what their child is doing in school, check on absences and dropouts, translating for elementary school parents and children." He had five cases of Lao dropouts, "three or four boys all get married, some sexy girl decides to go somewhere else and not attend school. Some marry, some [have] family problems." Bounmy said his best work is when "I [get] people back [in] school." He summarized the problems for Laotians and Cambodians: "The process of Americaniz[ing], [they] go American too fast, but they don't know what American is. The language may look like it, but kids don't know what's going on, how to get a job, high school requirements. Kids don't know what is going on, [they] don't know anything about college."

The Cambodian vocational resource teacher said that problems are greater for Cambodians. She said Cambodian youngsters "are disturbed within themselves. There are teen dropouts—both boys and girls. Parents don't know how to help. Students don't want to study. Sometimes [there is] fighting at bus stops when students wait too long." A Lao social worker said that "some Lao children tried to play the role of parents because parents work during the morning and at night. Parents have no time for their children. Their children have bad friends."

Child abuse also had become a problem for all of the groups (including the Hmong) and bruises from it were showing up in gym classes. One of the concerns in the Hmong community was the frustration that elders felt when they did not know how to help their children. The executive director of the Hmong-Lao Unity Association said the Hmong do not understand "mental health," but some are depressed and under a lot of stress.

Obstacles Faced by the Paraprofessionals

Initially, the Southeast Asian paraprofessional counselors were not recognized as a resource by the teachers, principals, or guidance counselors. They were given their space and allowed to do whatever they chose as long as they did not bother anyone. The paraprofessionals complained that by the time the guidance counselors referred a student to them, it was too late. They had already dropped out, or failed their courses, or done whatever the counselors were supposed to help them avoid. The paraprofessionals also complained that they were seeing Southeast Asians in isolation. In order to be able to assess the behavior of Southeast Asian students, they wanted to have access to other students, not just ESL students.

The Southeast Asian counselors recognized that they needed more training to meet the needs of students. One paraprofessional said he wanted to know about the "real thing counselor, what is it?" They all wanted hands-on training that would guide them in the basic needs of students, provide them with tools like note-taking skills, and give them some background in trauma counseling, job counseling, and student parenting. They did not envision the training as part of a degree program necessarily, but they expected that they would earn credits they could use later toward master's degrees in counseling.

The Southeast Asian paraprofessionals hoped that special training would give them some leverage so that the school guidance counselors and teachers would respect them. Politically, they felt it was important to show the state's department of education that they were receiving training and earning credit toward becoming certified counselors, "because," as the director of the Hmong-Lao Unity

Association said, "we don't know how they are going to turn us down." They hoped that the state would either recognize their position or provide an alternative route by which they could help the school staff meet the needs of Southeast Asian students.

The paraprofessionals wanted workshops that would bring in experts for both the Southeast Asian community and the teachers and counselors, but it had to be clear that the Southeast Asians controlled these workshops. They also wanted more interaction with principals. This is the Hmong strategy: to align with power. As one of the Hmong leader pointed out, the paraprofessionals had no authority to recruit or provide counseling on their own. They wanted to have small group meetings with the principal, teachers, and counselors to share materials and experiences, and to discuss problems and success stories. Someone suggested that distributing booklets produced by the paraprofessionals to parents, teachers, and guidance counselors would ease interaction. The local community foundation strongly recommended a citizen advisory group to advise the three counselors about maneuvering through Milltown politics.

The Ford Foundation agreed to provide funding for the training of the paraprofessionals so that they could upgrade their credentials in counseling and so that they could better "advise principals, counselors, and teachers to better understand and more sensitively help Southeast Asian students and, also, . . . advise Southeast Asian parents to better understand the public schools and how they can help their children." Chief Program Officer Edward Meade pointed out that it was impossible for three individuals to serve all of the Southeast Asians in the Milltown schools. To maximize effectiveness, he suggested the three become "counselor advisers" for non–Southeast Asian teachers, counselors, and administrators so that the schools could better serve the needs of their students. In this light, the assignment of the paraprofessionals would become "to assist and advise school guidance counselors and school teachers rather than to act exclusively as caseworkers who are assigned individual students to counsel."

A center for evaluation and research at a nearby college was asked to design and implement a training program for the paraprofessionals. As an established and professionally respected organization, the center gave the Southeast Asian paraprofessionals some status. The center put together a model training program and recommendations for recruitment, training plans, and sources of future funding to support the paraprofessional program. It brought Milltown administrators and the teachers' union into the discussion of the role of the paraprofessionals. The end result was that in the following year, the school department embraced the paraprofessionals and paid their salaries.

A Bridge Between Two Worlds

In light of the increasing tensions between the two worlds that exist for Hmong youngsters—the world of the Hmong community and that of the American teenager—which have been described in previous chapters, the need for bicultural guidance becomes obvious. Joua Kue, the Hmong home liaison in Milltown explained:

> The teacher and the counselors, they don't work together. There is no counselor to direct them to certain needs, they don't have people to advise them that this is good for you, that is good for you. They don't deem your child as important. . . . If the child doesn't speak up, the child who may not know what they are going to do, to apply to any schools, to choose a major. Maybe they don't even know what this is about. If you have only x [number of] students in the college program, it means nothing. [It] doesn't mean that they can all go through or they know what they need or what they are. They need someone there, Cambodian or Hmong or Laotian, who can [tell them] what they need to study and what grade they need to improve their education, so we need both a professional and someone to teach them for college.

An administrator of the Office of Bilingual Education in Milltown said that there is "a screaming, urgent and unmet need" for more staff in the Milltown schools to work with the Southeast Asians. An elementary principal in Milltown said, "In high school, if the parents don't keep a firm eye on it, the kids are going to choose the easiest courses, and they're not going to be educated for anything. I say to my sixth graders, you want to get into 'Times 2' if you want to go to college. You want to get into 'Times 2' if you want to be an engineer. You don't just want to take dance and drama."

Milltown is not the only place needing Southeast Asian counselors. Hmong youth in Oregon often told Cohn (1986) that they needed counseling in school. Goldstein (1985), found that Hmong students in Wisconsin have no one to direct them or to counsel them. One Hmong girl in high school said, "Nobody can help yourself to decision. You have to help yourself everything" (Goldstein, 1985, p. 265).

Bicultural counselors are needed in all stages of the school system—elementary, middle, and high school. Parents and students need access to someone who works in the schools who understands their culture and background and speaks their language. Students may require help for post-traumatic stress, incorrect grade placement, acculturation difficulties, tensions between home and school cultures, low self-esteem and expectations, preparation for college or work, and finding a homework partner or group that offers support to a student learning English.

The Stockton Massacre

There is a need for paraprofessional guidance counselors everywhere that there are Southeast Asian students. The killing of five Southeast Asian elementary school children in Stockton, California, in January 1989 by a young European American dressed in army fatigues raised many questions about the preparation that existing school counselors receive to allow them to deal with even the day-to-day problems in school districts that have large numbers of Southeast Asian students. As Kam (1989, p. 8) wrote,

> No one can say for sure what motivated Patrick Purdy, a young white drifter with a history of mental problems, to vent his rage upon four hundred elementary school children before shooting himself through the head. Some believe racism drove him; others think he was too crazed to care what color his victims were. Purdy's bullets struck children of various races. But because four of the slain were Cambodian, one Vietnamese, and the majority of the twenty-nine injured students were also Southeast Asians, Purdy's 106 rounds of fire ripped into the psyches of a refugee people who had already suffered some of the worst mass atrocities in recent history.

In Stockton, few if any counselors were prepared to help the families and classmates of the slain children because they had no background in Southeast Asian cultures. How many of the counselors knew about Buddhism or the animistic beliefs of rural Cambodians, Lao, and Hmong? While few would ever have the opportunity to visit a Southeast Asian village, they would have benefited from visiting the homes of Southeast Asian families in the United States.

An administrator for the Stockton Unified School District said that many of the counselors were "arrogant and pompous" as they persistently knocked on the doors of the homes of slain children and insisted on being allowed in. The counselors did not ask Southeast Asians what they should do; they told them, and "then they wondered why they had difficulty getting through." These individuals may have meant well, but because they lacked preparation, some may have made things worse. The superintendent wanted teachers trained to make home visits, but the administrator argued that they were not even prepared to teach in their classrooms. From another point of view, the home visits might have benefited the teachers most.

The havoc wreaked by one man in army fatigues, who killed four Cambodian children and one Vietnamese child and wounded twenty-nine others, galvanized the Stockton community briefly and brought to the attention of the nation the situation of Southeast Asians in American schools. But by and large, the media coverage ignored the fact that on a day-to-day basis, the concerns, tensions, questions, and need for academic and social counseling of Southeast Asian youngsters by bicultural counselors in elementary, middle, and high schools as well as colleges across the country are ignored. That situation was well expressed by a Vietnamese mother of two elementary children in Los Angeles who testified before a hearing on immigrant students sponsored by the National Coalition of Advocates for Students (NCAS) in 1987:

> My first observation is there has been a very limited communication between the parents and the school. Second observation is the Vietnamese students, like any other immigrant student populations, need help to understand the educational system to prepare themselves for higher education. They also need help to overcome the difficulties in the social, psychological, educational adjustments in which they themselves are pretty much alone because they do not find support services from the school system. Their own parents are still struggling to survive in the first years of their new experience in this land. More personnel [are] needed to provide professional support service to the students, to help them overcome two things: the adjustment that they have to make in language and education, and social and psychological adjustment. At this time I don't believe that the school systems do provide sufficient support to the students.

Recommendations for Action

During my research for the NCAS study, I visited with students in their homes. What two students in particular told me highlighted the need for bicultural counselors. The first of the two children was a Hmong boy in Milltown who said he was fifteen years old by his count and was put in sixth grade. He said he did not want the other children to know about his past because "they are too young." Milltown children picked on him on the bus and in his homeroom, but he said, "They are children." He said there was no one in his elementary school to help him with his schoolwork, and no one at home to help him.

As he talked, his grandfather watched, dressed in traditional costume with a small black beany-type cap, a short black jacket, and baggy pants. His grandfather did not understand English and had never had any formal education, but as the eldest of the family household, he was the leader and thereby expected to direct his grandson's progression to adulthood. Several younger children ran around as the boy talked and the grandfather looked on. When the other children are the boy's age, they will probably turn to him for help, not to the grandfather. He is the groundbreaker in his family.

What a Hmong bicultural counselor could do in this situation would be to suggest that the boy's guidance counselor move him into a middle school, if there is one, or into the seventh grade, so he would be in a junior high school with other Hmong and students closer to his age. A counselor might suggest forming groups of students to work together on their homework with the assistance of someone older who has a better command of academic English. The bicultural counselor could counsel small groups of students with unusual backgrounds. She or he could talk to the boy's teachers to help them understand his and other Hmong students' behavior in school.

The other student I visited was a fourteen-year-old Hmong girl who had arrived in Milltown from Thailand nine months before.

She lived in a two-bedroom apartment with eight other people in a wooden triple-decker near the interstate highway. When we talked, the shades were drawn, and the living room was dark, like the main room in Hmong homes in northern Thailand and in the Ban Vinai refugee camp. Blia Xiong was dressed in her best dress, a well-worn red chiffon dress with bows someone had probably given her. She wore plastic thongs on her feet. Her hair was pulled back in a pony tail that had never been cut—evidence that she was not married. Her mother made her sit in a straight-back chair directly in front of me. I sat on the couch. There was no other furniture in the room. Her younger siblings circled around her as she squirmed, wrung her hands, chewed her lips, and looked out of the corners of her eyes to avoid looking in my eyes.

Blia was ten years old when she first attended school. She attended primary school at Ban Vinai Refugee camp for three years and the Preparation for American Secondary Schools (PASS) program for six months. When Blia arrived in the United States in January 1986, she was placed in the seventh grade at a local middle school. There were three other Hmong in her class. She was given a test of what she described as "pictures" and passed from seventh to eighth grade even though her understanding of English was negligible. She struggled to understand me, but could not.

Through an interpreter, Blia said she had two teachers. One taught math and English and one taught "pictures." I asked if she meant reading. She said she did not know. The seventh-grade teacher did not help her. When she went to her for help, the teacher would say, "Go sit down." I asked her to tell me exactly what she said to the teacher. In English she said, "I don't know this one can you help me?" Apparently, she had learned this line in the PASS program in Thailand. She had also been told to ask for help when she did not understand. Blia said she asks for help four or five times a day. No one in her home speaks English, so there is no one to help her with her homework. Her Hmong friend at school helps her and teaches her.

Blia said she did not know if she had a counselor. She did not know if she would graduate. She did not want a job. Her mother said if she were at Ban Vinai, they would be looking for someone for her to marry. Blia said she did not know if it was important for girls to be successful. Her mother defined success for a girl as going to school so she can learn how to choose a husband. Her mother had left her husband behind at Ban Vinai refugee camp in Thailand, probably with another wife. She seemed bitter. Like most Hmong women, she had probably married when she was very young. She hoped that by being educated her daughter would have more power over her decision.

In this case, a bicultural counselor could help Blia join a group that would help her with her homework and her English. The most useful thing a bicultural counselor could do would be to provide insight into the American educational system and American cultural expectations for teenage girls. If the bicultural counselor were an educated Hmong woman, she could provide Blia with a new role model. As with the boy, a bicultural counselor could help Blia's teachers to understand her better and better meet her needs. Why did one teacher always tell her to sit down? Was it because Blia did not understand the culture of the classroom and was disrupting a lesson? Was it because Blia did not understand English and the teacher needed a Hmong aide to translate for her? Was it because the teacher was tired or overworked? Was it because the teacher was racist? Was it for another reason?

Southeast Asian students interviewed for the NCAS Immigrant Student project usually did not know who their guidance counselors were. They turned to ESL or bilingual teachers to act as counselors. In some school districts, like Seattle, a Lao aide was the ex officio counselor for all Southeast Asian students in the junior high where he worked, but he received no remuneration or status for his work.

An eighteen-year-old Hmong boy in St. Paul, Minnesota, wanted to go to college. He had a counselor, but no knowledge of the SAT or other college requirements. The need for counselors to explain to students what is necessary to apply to college is not specific to the Hmong. A Cambodian senior at a vocational technical school in Massachusetts said she wanted to go to college. No one told her that the vocational technical track is an alternative to college. A fourteen-year-old Lao girl in Houston was interested in becoming a teacher, but her guidance counselor had not helped her begin select college-preparation-level classes.

Older Cambodian youngsters who were separated from their families during the Pol Pot regime in 1975 to 1979 and younger Cambodians whose families have broken apart in the United States after so many years of trauma may need culturally sensitive counseling. I asked a seventeen-year-old Cambodian young man in Milltown what he learned when he was separated from his family and attended "school" during the Pol Pot regime. His eyes filled with anguish, he leaned across the table and looked at me evenly, uncharacteristic for a Cambodian, and said, "You don't want to know." A seventeen-year-old Cambodian girl student in Lowell, Massachusetts, who I had known for eight years, erased the years 1975 to 1979 from her life history; when I asked her about these years, she said she could not remember what she did.

Vietnamese youngsters who escaped by boat were among the most brutalized of refugees because of the pirates they encountered. Many of the girls were raped, sometimes repeatedly. A very intelligent fourteen-year-old Vietnamese boy in Boston surprised me when I asked him if his escape had been difficult. He said, "It was fair." An elementary school principal in Chelsea, Massachusetts, told me about a young Vietnamese boy whose mother had said they had had a difficult escape. His teacher sent him to her office. The principal asked him about his behavior. He said that "when he gets angry, he gets a headache and [he says] his spirit is going to die, so the teacher has no right to make him angry." Then he asked the principal an unsettling question, "Don't you know this is the house of freedom?" I told the principal that work by Coles (1986) suggests that many children who have experienced war have been politicized and are frustrated as they try to integrate their pasts with their new lives. She said, "That's the problem, we're trying to find ways to understand them; it's like a whole other world, and we're trying to mainstream them." She had referred this child for special education. She said, "He was really out of it, I could tell."

This same principal was surprised to learn that more than half of the Cambodian high school students in Chelsea had been referred for special education. I visited the special education "classroom" in the Chelsea elementary school. It was a small converted storage room. All but one of the children appeared to be severely handicapped. The one exception was a pretty Cambodian girl. I wondered who had classified her for special education.

Another example of a youngster who obviously needed someone to talk to who understood his past was a high school ESL student in Colorado. The teacher had arranged his students in rows by ability and placed three students, two Hmong who had just arrived from the camps and a Cambodian boy, in the next room with an aide. They were connecting dots. As soon as I entered the room, the Cambodian boy started talking. During the ten minutes I was in the room he never stopped talking. In flawless English, he told me that everyone in his family was dead but his mother and him. He was afraid his mother was going to die because she was so sad, she did not want to live. He did not know what to do about his mother. The boy's English ability indicated that he was bright. I wondered why he was in the "connect the dots" class and who was at the school to help him?

Parents want someone at the school they can talk to, too. A Lao father in Long Beach, California, made two appointments in the elementary school to talk about his son, but he did not fully understand the teacher (National Coalition of Advocates for Students, 1988). The father said he did not know enough about the school system to know if his child was being guided properly. He had no education before refugee camp. A Vietnamese mother in Amherst,

Massachusetts, said, "Being a parent with limited English-speaking skill, I feel that I am being deprived of my rights as a parent whenever I am in need of questioning my child's performance." In the elementary system her child is attending, "there is no adult where my child can come to receive the help which he needed" (testimony at public hearing, Boston, 1986, in preparation for the National Coalition of Advocates for Students 1988 report).

The advantages of having a bilingual, bicultural counselor are not only for the students, but for the parents as well. Brighton, Massachusetts, had a Vietnamese ESL high school teacher who had been certified because she had taught in Vietnam. As in Southeast Asia, when she ran into her students' mothers at the market or on the street, they invited her over for tea and to discuss their childrens' performance informally. Her Vietnamese students often visited the teacher at her home.

One example of the advantages of a bilingual, bicultural staff was a fifteen-year-old boy who recently arrived from Vietnam. Four hours a day he was in the ESL 1 class with the Vietnamese teacher. She knew he was "very intelligent" because she could speak to him in Vietnamese. He spoke to her in Vietnamese about problems he had in English. He also felt comfortable talking to his guidance counselor in Vietnamese. The Vietnamese guidance counselor also made it easy for his parents to communicate with the school.

The lessons learned from the bicultural paraprofessional counselors model is that there is a great need for people in the schools who not only can speak to the students and their parents in their first language but also can share similar life experiences and class backgrounds. There is a further need for these individuals to work with teachers and existing guidance counselors as well.

Risk and Trust

In the words of Frederick Erickson (1987, p. 344): "To learn is to entertain risk, since learning involves moving just past the level of competence, what is already mastered, to the nearest region of incompetence, what has not yet been mastered." An analogy to rock climbing is useful. You cannot go any higher than your abilities; each foot and finger placement enables the next. You also cannot go any further than you trust your abilities, your equipment, and your partner, so that if you fall, you will be held by the rope attached to your partner's waist. There is risk involved for all students and climbers.

In Vygotsky's "zone of proximal development" theory, there is a region where a student can function not yet alone but with a more competent partner (Vygotsky, 1978, pp. 84–91; Erickson, 1987, p. 344). Many youngsters need to test the competency of their teacher as a partner before they will trust the teacher to take them into a new field of knowledge. In many successful cases, the teacher is a special, caring individual who understands the learner's limitations and strengths, and builds on those strengths while providing confidence to overcome limitations. According to Erickson, to accomplish this "it is essential that the teacher and students establish and maintain trust in each other at the edge of risk. . . . Schools are one arena where we can work to change the existing distributions of power and knowledge in our society" (Erickson, 1987, pp. 344, 352).

My recommendation is to be aggressively multicultural. Treating our national wealth of diversity in cultures and languages as a strength will serve us far better than regarding it as a weakness. Recent immigrants bring the aspirations and determination that all new immigrants have brought to this country. Careful nurturing of these hopes and aspirations in our schools could foster critical and creative thinkers who will lead the United States into the twenty-first century.

⊚⊚
Epilogue

This book has been about the other side of the amazing Asian American academic success story. It has been about the broad challenges to providing an equal educational opportunity to Southeast Asian students when, for example, there are not enough credentialed teachers who speak these languages. It has used the Hmong as a case study of the extent of the challenges facing schools as they enter the twenty-first century. It has provided a historical backdrop to show that first U.S. foreign policy of the 1960s and 1970s and then U.S. immigration policies of the 1960s, 1970s, and 1980s created the challenge we now face of educating Southeast Asian refugee students, and we must now face up to the solutions. The bitter medicine required will call for new strategies, the questioning of easy formulas, and a reconsideration of what American public education is, what purposes it serves, and ultimately, who we are as Americans.

As I have tried to point out, the current system of educating newcomer students from Southeast Asian backgrounds is not working for the Southeast Asians, and it is not serving society in general. We must ultimately recognize that "them" is "us." Investment in the education of newcomers is investment in the economic prosperity of this country in the next century. Historically, Americans have always feared that immigrants would pauperize this country. We have also feared that immigrants would not be loyal to democracy.

Education is one way to prevent this from happening, but we continue to be reluctant to invest in education the amount of resources necessary to make it work. We will all benefit by giving more financial resources to schools to reduce the size of classes, better educate teachers, and provide career ladders for bicultural classroom aides and paraprofessional counselors.

I began this book by talking about the myth that Asian Americans are so successful academically that they do not need special attention in school. I did my best to dismantle the concept that Asian Americans exist as a monolithic group. Next, I demonstrated the similarities in the experiences of school districts that serve Hmong and other Southeast Asian students by comparing two seemingly disparate school districts at opposite ends of the country, one rural and one urban. I then addressed the challenges of cultural influences on learning, highlighting gender-related issues among the Hmong and presenting a theoretical framework for educators to better understand the importance of survival and how the drive to survive mitigates the validity of motivation theories. I then broadened my focus to the systematic problems of the programs offered to Southeast Asian students and found that the inadequacies of these varied programs are frighteningly similar. Family-based multicultural education was presented as one alternative, along with a model program for paraprofessional bicultural counselors that showed what can be done when the community, schools, and funding sources come together.

I would like to close this book by connecting the lessons learned from the Hmong with systematic problems and systematic solutions. Every Asian American culture is as distinct in its own way as the Hmong. No assumptions can be made purely on the basis of categorical race. As with all newcomers, the Hmong are changing so rapidly that by the time this book is published it will not apply to all Hmong, especially those who have defied all odds and are academically successful.

It's Not the Methods That Count

The most important point I want to make is that it is not the methods that count in determining the academic success of Hmong students; it is the teacher-student and the home–school relationships. This lesson goes beyond the Hmong; it includes all Southeast Asian students and other English-learning newcomers. Teachers spend too much time trying to learn new methods to teach students who are learning English, and too little time learning from the students themselves. Building solid teacher-student and home–school relationships takes commitment on the part of both teachers and learners to learn about one another. It will take federal money to reduce the financial burden on states to make the size of classrooms uniformly smaller so that teachers have the time and space to develop this relationship, and to provide ongoing teacher in-service workshops and better multicultural preparation for pre-service teachers.

The basic hypothesis of this book is that when we think about immigrant students we must think about families, not just about individual students. The academic success of newcomer students requires considerable sacrifices on the part of their families. This is particularly true for Hmong and other Southeast Asians who come from homes with traditional gender divisions of labor. In order to support these students' success in this country, educators need to have knowledge about the importance of survival to their students' families, to make efforts to connect home and school learning, and to reorder classroom objectives and expectations in response to family survival demands.

This book advocates replacing the deficit theory that overshadows ESL and Sheltered English programs with a family-based multicultural educational theory. Students who speak another language better than English should be referred to as learners of English rather than as limited-English-proficient students. Students who are learning English require small, multicultural classes that are integrated with primary English-speaking students. Instead of teaching English as a Second Language or simplified English in Sheltered English classes, the new approach calls for students to actually be taught English, as distinct from Language Arts. These English classes should focus on writing nativelike English and learning English grammar and syntax. They should aim to raise levels of interpretive and comprehension skills. They should not simplify English or concepts. They should work on concept development specifically, rather than implicitly. They should also develop standardized test-taking skills. The goal of these classes should be to connect existing skills and knowledge to English, not to replicate skill development. Parents and other bicultural and bilingual aides should be available in every classroom in which the teacher does not understand the first language of students. All programs should have definable strategies. The programs should be monitored by bilingual evaluators. The results of these programs should be measured against alternative programs.

In addition, special programs should be organized by the schools and culturally based mutual assistance agencies to provide bilingual support classes before or after school or on Saturdays for students needing support with English or just help doing their homework. The U.S. Department of Education must become more involved in the daily expenses of providing for more classroom aides as well as in-service training for those aides. It must support the provision of career ladders for classroom aides who want to become bilingual teachers, and the improvement of preparation for teachers in training. It must also provide ongoing in-service training in family-based multicultural education for teachers. Teachers require ongoing monthly workshops on culture and language orchestrated with local community organizations. They need to be taught how to help raise expectations for students who do not share their home language or cultural backgrounds. They need to understand what it takes to build confidence in a new language, rather than cause a loss of confidence by simplifying language and content. Most importantly, teachers have to do away with the deficit perspective by identifying cultural strengths and weaknesses of their students.

In summary, an adequate response to the challenges presented by Southeast Asian students should entail rethinking national and state policies, school programs for students who are learning English, and teacher education regarding multicultural education. The most important thing that the federal government can do is provide more financial support to states and to particular school districts that have large numbers of immigrant and refugee students. Both good financial sense and common sense suggest that the federal government also should streamline participation in the educational programs offered to refugees, beginning with those programs offered in refugee camps by the Department of State, followed by the adult and family education offered by the Office of Refugee Resettlement of the Department of Health and Human Services, and finally, the programs offered to schools by the Department of Education for refugee and immigrant students.

Assessing Programs

The following questions may help schools assess how they are meeting the educational challenges presented by Hmong and other Southeast Asian students. The questions are straightforward, but the answers may be surprising. The questions are arranged according to issues concerning the school plant, integration, the teaching staff, the curriculum and teaching materials, students, parents, and community.

Where are English-learning students in the school plant? Are they all in certain classrooms? Where are those classrooms located in relation to the administrative offices? Is there a place for pregnant girls and young mothers with babies?

In what tracks or levels of classes do you find most newcomer students? How are English-learning students integrated in the

school? What is taught in ESL programs? Are all subject materials covered in these classes? In what classes do students learn
grammar, English syntax, decontextualizing skills and test-
taking skills?

What positions do Southeast Asian adults and adults from other
language groups hold in the schools? What is being done to
upgrade those positions? Are these individuals regarded as
resources for the teachers? Does the teacher acknowledge and
use the skills developed by the Hmong and other cultures?

What is taught and how is it taught? Are the textbooks, tests
or testing procedures, and classroom discussions based on
implicit assumptions of culture and background that may
exclude newcomers like the Hmong? Have Hmong and other
newcomer students been involved in developing materials?

How welcome do parents feel coming to the school? How much
interaction is there between the community and the school?
Are parents regarded as a resource or as a problem? Is their culture viewed as a strength in the school, as a challenge, or as a
problem?

References

Arnold, F., Minocha, U., and Fawcett, J. "The Changing Face of Asian Immigration to the United States." In J. Fawcett and B. Carino (eds.), *Pacific Bridges: The New Immigration from Asia and the Pacific Islands*. Staten Island: Center for Migration Studies, 1987, pp. 105–152.

Barney, G. L. "The Meo of Xieng Kouang Province, Laos." In Peter Kunstadter (ed.), *Southeast Asian Tribes, Minorities, and Nations*. Princeton University Press, 1967. (Originally published 1957.)

Blanchard, J., and Horn, L. *Report of Survey of Refugee Needs and Problems in Ban Vinai Refugee Camp*. Bangkok: Catholic Organization for Emergency Relief and Refugees, 1986.

Bliatout, B. T., Downing, B., Lewis, J., and Yang, D. *Handbook for Teaching Hmong-Speaking Students*. Rancho Cordova, Calif.: Southeast Asian Community Resource Center, Folsom Cordova Unified School District, 1988.

Boothby, N. "Unaccompanied Children in Emergencies: A Psychological Perspective." Unpublished qualifying paper, Graduate School of Education, Harvard University, 1982.

Boothby, N. "The Care and Placement of Unaccompanied Children in Emergencies." Unpublished doctoral dissertation, Graduate School of Education, Harvard University, 1984.

Brand, D. "The New Whiz Kids: Why Asian Americans Are Doing So Well, and What It Costs Them." *Time Magazine*, August 31, 1987.

Brandon, P. R. "Gender Differences in Educational Attainment Among Asian Americans in the High-School and Beyond: Senior Cohort Third Follow-up Survey." Paper presented to the annual meeting of the American Educational Research Association, Boston, 1990.

Butler, J., and Thompson, D. "Updating Knowledge of Cultural Journalism Projects Among Secondary Schools Across the Country." Paper presented to the AEJMC midwinter meeting, New Orleans, January, 1990.

Butterfield, F. "Why Asians Are Going to the Head of the Class." In "Education Life" section, *New York Times*, August 3, 1986.

California Department of Education. *Fact Book, 1993–1994*. Sacramento: California Department of Education, 1994.

Caplan, N., Whitmore, J., and Bui, Q. "Southeast Asian Refugee Self-Sufficiency Study." Final report to the Office of Refugee Resettlement, Washington, D.C., January 1985.

Caplan, N., Whitmore, J., Bui, Q., and Trautman, M. "Study Shows Boat Refugees' Children Achieve Academic Success." *Refugee Reports*, October 11, 1985, pp. 1–6.

Caplan, N., Whitmore, J., and Choy, M. *The Boat People and Achievement in America*. Ann Arbor: University of Michigan Press, 1989.

Caplan, N., Choy, M., and Whitmore, J. *Children of the Boat People: A Study of Educational Success*. Ann Arbor: University of Michigan Press, 1991.

Caplan, N., Choy, M., and Whitmore, J. "Indochinese Refugee Families and Academic Achievement." *Scientific American*, February 1992, pp. 36–42.

Carino, B. V. "The Philippines and Southeast Asia: Historical Roots and Contemporary Linkages." In J. Fawcett and B. Carino (eds.), *Pacific Bridges: The New Immigration from Asia and the Pacific Islands*. Staten Island: Center for Migration Studies, 1987, pp. 305–326.

Cazdan, C., Carrasco, R., Maldonado-Guzman, A. A., and Erickson, F. "The Contribution of Ethnographics Research to Bicultural Bilingual Education." In James Atlatis, (ed.) *Georgetown University Round Table on Language and Linguistics 1980*. Washington, D.C.: Georgetown University Press, 1980.

Chan, S. *The Bitter Sweet Soil*. Berkeley, Calif.: University of California Press, 1986.

Chun, K. "The Myth of Asian American Success and Its Educational Ramifications." *IRCD Bulletin*, 1980, 15(1–2), 1–12.

Chuong, H. C., and Van, L. *The Amerasians from Vietnam: A California Study*. Folsom, Calif.: Southeast Asia Community Resource Center, 1994.

Cohn, M. "Hmong Adolescents." In B. Downing and D. Olney (eds.), *The Hmong in Transition*. Staten Island, N.Y.: Center for Migration Studies, 1986, 197–202.

Coles, R. *The Political Life of Children*. Boston: Atlantic Monthly Press, 1986.

Cooper, R. *Resource Scarcity and the Hmong Response*. Singapore University Press, 1984., 261–262.

Crystal, E., and Saepharn, K. "Iu-Mien: Highland Southeast Asian Community and Culture in a California Context." In J. Lewis (ed.), *Minority Cultures of Laos*. Rancho Cordova, Calif.: Southeast Asia Community Resource Center, Folsom Cordova Unified School District, 1992, pp. 327–401.

Cumming, B. J. "The Development of Attachment in Two Groups of Economically Disadvantaged Infants and their Mothers: Hmong Refugee and Caucasian-American." Unpublished doctoral dissertation, Graduate School, University of Minnesota, 1988.

Cummins, J. "The Influence of Bilingualism on Cognitive Growth: A Synthesis of Research Findings and Exploratory Hypotheses." *Working Papers on Bilingualism*, 1976, 9, 1–43.

Cummins, J. *Bilingualism and Special Education: Issues in Assessment and Pedagogy*. Avon, UK: Multilingual Matters Ltd., 1984.

Curtain, P. "Migration in the Tropical World." In V. Yans-McLaughlin (ed.), *Immigration Reconsidered*. New York: Oxford University Press, 1990.

Daniels, R. *Asian America: Chinese and Japanese in the United States Since 1850*. Seattle: University of Washington Press, 1988.

Dillin, J. "Asian-Americans: The Soaring Minority." *The Christian Science Monitor*, October, 1985.

Dunnigan, T. "Segmentary Kinship in an Urban Society: The Hmong of St. Paul." *Anthropological Quarterly*, 1982, 55(3).

Erickson, F. "Culture and Science Education." *The Urban Review*, 1986, 18(2), 117–124.

Erickson, F. "Transformation and School Success: The Politics and Culture of Educational Achievement." In *Anthropology and Education Quarterly*, 1987, 18(4), 335–356.

Farley, R., and Neidert, L. "How Effective Was the Melting Pot?" Research Report (84–68), Population Studies Center, University of Michigan, December 1984.

Felsman, J. K., Johnson, M., Felsman, I., and Leong, F. "AmerAsians at Risk in Public Schools?" In D. Ranard and D. Gilzow (eds.). "The AmerAsians." *In America Perspectives on Refugee Resettlement*, June 1989, Refugee Service Center, Center for Applied Linguistics.

Fix, M., and Passel, J. S. *Immigration and Immigrants: Setting the Record Straight*. Washington, D.C.: The Urban Institute, 1994.

Fordham, S., and Ogbu, J. "Black Students' School Success: Coping with the 'Burden of Acting White.'" In *Urban Review*, 1986, 18(3), 176–206.

Freeman, D., and Freeman, Y. "Sheltered English Instruction." *ERIC Digest*,

ED301070, Office of Educational Research and Improvement, Washington, D.C., October 1988.

Gardner, R. C., and Lambert, W. E. *Attitudes and Motivation in Second Language Learning.* Rowley, Mass.: Newbury House, 1972.

Geddes, W. *Migrants of the Mountain: The Cultural Ecology of the Blue Miao (Hmong Njua) of Thailand.* London: Oxford University Press, 1976.

Gee, J. P. "Orality and Literacy: From the Savage Mind to Ways with Words." *TESOL Quarterly,* 1986.

Geertz, C. *The Interpretation of Cultures.* New York: Basic Books, 1973.

Goldstein, B. L. "Schooling for Cultural Transitions: Hmong Girls and Boys in American High Schools." Unpublished doctoral dissertation, School of Education, University of Wisconsin, Madison, 1985.

Greer, C. *The Great School Legend: A Revisionist Interpretation of American Public Education.* New York: Basic Books, 1972.

Grimes, B. (ed.). *Ethnologue: Languages of the World.* (11th ed.) Dallas: Summer Institute of Languages, 1988.

Hakuta, K. *Mirrors of Language: The Debate on Bilingualism.* New York: Basic Books, 1986.

Hakuta, K., and Snow, C. "The Role of Research in Policy Decisions About Bilingual Education." *National Association of Bilingual Education News,* 1986, *IX*(3).

Halberstam, D. *The Best and the Brightest.* New York: Random House, 1972.

Hein, J. *States and International Migrants: The Incorporation of Indochinese Refugees in the United States and France.* San Francisco: Westview Press, 1993.

Herrnstein, R. J., and Murray, C. *The Bell Curve: Intelligence and Class Structure in American Life.* New York: The Free Press, 1994.

Hersh, S. M. *The Price of Power: Kissinger in the Nixon White House.* New York: Summit Books, 1983.

Hirano-Nakanishi, M. "It Ain't Necessarily So." Paper presented at the Annual Meeting of the American Educational Research Association, San Francisco, Calif., April 1992.

History–Social Science Curriculum Framework and Criteria Committee, *History–Social Science Framework for the California Public Schools Kindergarten Through Grade Twelve.* Adopted by the California State Board of Education in July 1987. California State Department of Education: 1988.

Hurh, W. M., and Kim, K. C. "The 'Success' Image of Asian Americans: Its Validity, and Its Practical and Theoretical Implications." *Ethnic and Racial Studies,* 1989, *12*(4), 512–38.

Huynh, D. T. "The Indochinese and Their Cultures." Multifunctional Resource

Center, Policy Studies Department, College of Education, San Diego State University, 1988.

Hvitfeldt, C. "Traditional Culture, Perceptual Style, and Learning: The Classroom Behavior of Hmong Adults." *Adult Education Quarterly*, 1986, 36(2), 65–77.

Ima, K. "How Useful Is the Question?" Paper presented to the Annual Meeting of the American Educational Research Association, San Francisco, Calif., April 1992.

Itzkoff, S. *The Decline of Intelligence in America*. Westport, Conn.: Praeger, 1994.

Jensen, A. "How Much Can We Boost IQ and Scholastic Achievement?" *Harvard Educational Review*, Winter 1969, pp. 1–123.

Johnson, G. "Learning Just How Little Is Known About the Brain." *New York Times*, October 23, 1994, p. E5.

Jumsai, M.L.M. *History of Laos*. Bangkok, Thailand: Chalermnit 1–2 Erawan Arcade, 1971.

Kagan, J., and others. "How Much Can We Boost IQ and Scholastic Achievement? A Discussion." *Harvard Educational Review*, Spring 1969, pp. 273–356.

Kagan, J. "The Realistic View of Biology and Behavior." *The Chronicle of Higher Education*, October 1994, p. A64.

Kam, K. "A False and Shattered Peace." *California Tomorrow*, 1989, 4(2–3), 8–21.

Kan, S., and Liu, W. T. In N. Toshida (ed.), *Issues in Asian and Pacific American Education*. Minn.: Asian and Pacific Learning Resource Center, 1986.

Korenbrot, C., Minkler, D., and Brindis, C. *Western Journal of Medicine*, 1988, 148, pp. 349–354.

Lai, M., and others. "Reading and Written Expression Performance of Ten Asian/Pacific Islander Ethnic Groups on the Eighth Grade California Assessment Program." Paper presented at the Annual Meeting of the American Educational Research Association, Boston, April 1990.

Lanauze, M., and Snow, C. "The Relation Between First- and Second-Language Writing Skills: Evidence from Puerto Rican Elementary School Children in the Mainland." Manuscript, Harvard Graduate School of Education, 1988.

LaVally, R. *Californians Together: Defining the State's Role in Immigration*. Sacramento: California Senate Office of Research, 1993.

Lee, J.F.J. (ed.). *Asian American Experiences in the United States*. McFarland, 1993.

Lightfoot, S. L. *Worlds Apart: Relationship Between Families and Schools*. New York: Basic Books, 1978.

Lockwood, H. "Support Services to Limited-English Proficient Khmer Students at Lowell High School." Unpublished Final Report by Metropolitan Indochinese Children and Adolescent Services, South Cove Community Health Center, 1985.

Luangpraseut, K., and others. *Handbook for Teaching Lao-Speaking Students*. Rancho Cordova, Calif.: Southeast Asia Community Resource Center, Folsom Cordova Unified School District, 1989.

Matisoff, J. A. "The Lahu People and Their Language." In J. Lewis (ed.), *Minority Cultures of Laos*. Rancho Cordova, Calif.: Southeast Asia Community Resource Center, Folsom Cordova Unified School District, 1992.

McCoy, A. W., Reed, C., and Adams, L. *The Politics of Heroin in Southeast Asia*. New York: HarperCollins, 1972.

McGinn, F. "Hmong Literacy Among Hmong Adolescents and the Use of Hmong Literacy During Resettlement." Unpublished doctoral dissertation, School of Education, University of San Francisco, May 1989.

McLaughlin, B., Minicucci, C., Nelson, B., and Parrish, T. *Meeting the Challenge of Language Diversity*. Vol. III: *An Evaluation of Programs for Pupils with Limited English Proficiency*. Berkeley, Calif.: BW Associates, 1992.

Mizokawa, D. "The Problem with Lumping Data." Paper presented at 1992 Annual Meeting of American Educational Association, San Francisco, Calif., April 1992.

Mizokawa, D., and Ryckman, D. "Interethnic and Gender Differences in the Causal Attributions of Minority Students." Paper presented at the Annual Meeting of the American Educational Research Association, Boston, 1990.

Moll, L. "Bilingual Classroom Studies and Community Analysis: Some Recent Trends. *Educational Researcher*, 1992, *21*(2), 20–24.

Moll, L., and Diaz, E. "Ethnographic Pedagogy: Promoting Effective Bilingual Instruction." Laboratory of Comparative Human Cognition, University of California, San Diego, 1982.

Mollica, R., Lavelle, J., Wyshak, G., and Coelho, R. "The Southeast Asian Psychiatry Patient: A Treatment Outcome Study." St. Elizabeth's Hospital, Brighton Marine Public Health Center, Brighton, Mass., 1986.

Mottin, J. *The History of the Hmong* (Meo.). Bangkok: Odeon Store, 1980.

National Coalition of Advocates for Students. *New Voices: Immigrant Students in U.S. Public Schools*. Boston: National Coalition of Advocates for Students, 1988.

National Educational Longitudinal Study of 1988. Reported in *Education Week*, February 27, 1991.

Northcutt, L., and Watson, D. *Sheltered English Teaching Handbook*. Carlsbad,

Calif.: Northcutt, Watson, Gonzales, 1986.

Ogbu, J. *Minority Education and Caste: The American System in Cross-Cultural Perspective.* New York: Academic Press, 1978.

Ogbu, J. "Variability of Minority School Performance: A Problem in Search of an Explanation." *Anthropology and Education Quarterly,* 1987, *18*(4), 312–334.

Ogbu, J. "Minority Status and Literacy in Comparative Perspective." *Daedalus,* 1990, *119*(2), 141–168.

Peal, E., and Lambert, W. E. "The Relation of Bilingualism to Intelligence." *Psychological Monographs,* 1962, *76*(27), 1–23.

Perlmann, J. *Ethnic Differences: Schooling and Social Structure Among Irish, Italians, Jews and Blacks in an American City, 1880–1935.* New York: Cambridge University, 1988.

Refugee Reports, XII(12), December 30, 1991, 1–2.

Rickenbach, R. Testimony in "Refugee and Civilian War Casualty Problems in Laos and Cambodia." Staff Report to the Senate Committee on the Judiciary, Subcommittee on Refugees and Escapees, 1970.

Rigdon, J. E. "Exploding Myth: Asian-American Youth Suffer a Rising Toll from Heavy Pressures." *Wall St. Journal,* July 10, 1991.

Roberts, S. "Amazing Asians: The Secret of Their Academic Success." *The Columbia Flier,* December 19, 1985.

Rumbaut, R., and Ima, K. *The Adaptation of Southeast Asian Refugee Youth: A Comparative Study.* Vols. I and II. Southeast Asian Refugee Youth Study, Department of Sociology, San Diego State University, December 1987.

Rumbaut, R., and Weeks, J. "Fertility and Adaptation: Indochinese Refugees in the United States." *International Migration Review,* 1986, *20*(2), 428–466.

Ryckman, D. B., and Mizokawa, D. T. "Attributional Patterns of Gifted Minority Students: Gender Differences." Paper presented at the Annual Meeting of the American Educational Research Association, Boston, 1990.

Samway, K. D. "Writers' Workshop and Children Acquiring English as a Nonnative Language." Program Information Guide (10). Washington, D.C.: National Clearinghouse for Bilingual Education, 1992.

Sanchez, F. "What Is Sheltered Instruction?" Hayward, Calif.: Alameda County Office of Education, July 1989.

Schein, L. "Popular Culture and the Production of Difference: The Miao and China." Unpublished doctoral dissertation, Department of Anthropology, University of California at Berkeley, 1993.

Smalley, W., Vang, C. K., and Yang, G. Y. *Mother of Writing: The Origin and Development of a Hmong Messianic Script.* Chicago: University of Chicago Press, 1990.

Snow, C. E. "The Development of Definitional Skill." Unpublished paper, n.d.a.

Snow, C. E. "The Rationale for Native Language Instruction in the Education of Language Minority Children: Evidence from Several Lines of Research." Unpublished paper, n.d.b.

Sonsalla, D. R. "A Comparative Case Study of Secondary School Programs for Hmong Refugee Students in the Minneapolis and St. Paul Schools." Ph.D. thesis, University of Minnesota, 1984.

Szymusiak, M. *The Stones Cry Out: A Cambodian Childhood, 1975–1980*. New York: Hill and Wang, 1986. (Translated from French.)

Takaki, R. *Strangers from a Different Shore*. Boston: Little, Brown, 1989.

Tayanin, D., and Vang, L. "From the Village to the City: The Changing Life of the Kammu." In J. Lewis (ed.), *Minority Cultures of Laos*. Rancho Cordova, Calif.: Southeast Asia Community Resource Center, Folsom Cordova Unified School District, 1992, 1–72.

Thao, C. "Hmong Customs of Marriage, Divorce, and the Rights of Married Women." In B. Johns and D. Stecker (eds.), *The Hmong World*. New Haven: Yale Center for International and Area Studies, 1986.

"The Triumph of Asian-Americans." *The New Republic*, July 15–21, 1985.

Thomas, W., and Znaniecki, F. *The Polish Peasant in Europe and America*. Urbana, Ill.: University of Illinois Press, 1984. (Originally published as "The Polish Peasant in Europe and America: Monograph of an Immigrant Group." Boston: Richard Badge, 1918–1920.)

Tsang, S.-L. "The Mathematics Achievement Characteristics of Asian-American Students." In R. R. Cocking and J. P. Mestre (eds.), *Linguistic and Cultural Influences on Learning Mathematics*. Hillsdale, N.J.: Lawrence Erlbaum, 1988.

U.S. Commission on Civil Rights. "Civil Rights Issues Facing Asian Americans in the 1990s." A Report of the United States Commission on Civil Rights, February 1992.

Vang, A. "A Descriptive Study of Academically Proficient Hmong High School Girl Dropouts." Unpublished doctoral dissertation, School of Education, University of San Francisco, 1992.

Vangay, J.V.N. *Hmong Parents' Cultural Attitudes and the Sex-Ratio Imbalance of Hmong Merced High School Graduates*. Merced, Calif.: Mong Pheng Community Incorporated, 1989.

Vangyi, X. V. "The Needs for the Education for Laotian Refugees." Paper presented at the First National Indochinese Conference, Santa Ana, Calif., May 8–9, 1980.

Visathep, C. "Biography." In *The Original Tracks*. Portland, Oreg.: Portland Fox-fire Project, 1984.

Vygotsky, L. S. *Mind in Society: The Development of Higher Psychological Processes*. M. Cole, V. John-Steiner, S. Scribner, and E. Souberman (eds.), 84–91. Cambridge: Harvard University Press, 1978.

Walker, W. "Challenges of the Hmong Culture: A Study of Teacher, Counselor and Administrator Training in a Time of Changing Demographics." Unpublished doctoral dissertation, Graduate School of Education, Harvard University, 1989.

Walker, W. "A Window into Their Lives: Teachers Learning from Student Writing." In J. Cabello (ed.), *California Perspectives*. San Francisco: California Tomorrow, 1990.

Walker, W. "Barriers for Teenage Refugee Women's Education in the United States: A Comparison of Hmong and Mien Hilltribe Women." Paper presented to the Annual Meeting of the American Educational Research Association, Chicago, 1991.

Walker, W., and Moffat, D. "Ban Vinai: A Changing World for Hmong Children." In *Cultural Survival*, 1986, *10*(4).

Walker, W., and Moffat, D. "Acculturation Is a Very Big Word." *Reports Magazine*, 1987, 26.

Walker-Moffat, W. "Recent Mexican Immigrant Women to the U.S.: Fertility Rates and Use of Public Services," Report to the Select Committee on Statewide Immigration Impact of the California State Assembly and the California Elected Women's Association for Education and Research: Sacramento, 1994.

Wigginton, E. *Sometimes a Shining Moment: The Foxfire Experience*. Garden City, New York: Anchor Books, 1986.

Wong Fillmore, L., and Valadez, C. "Teaching Bilingual Learners." In M. C. Wittrock (ed.), *Handbook of Research on Teaching*. New York: Macmillan, 1987.

Worldwinds, 1982, *1*(1). Published as a special project of the Center for Studies in English as a Second Language, Boulder High School, Boulder, Col.

Yang, D. "The Hmong: Enduring Traditions." In J. Lewis (ed.), *Minority Cultures of Laos*. Rancho Cordova, Calif.: Southeast Asia Community Resource Center, Folsom Cordova Unified School District, 1992.

Yang, S. K. *The Hmong of Laos: 1896–1978*. Indochinese Refugee Education Guides. General Information Series No. 16. National Indochinese Clearinghouse, Center for Applied Linguistics, 1981.

Index